Dating After The Red Pill

By Stevan Terzić

ISBN: 9798648054738

Legal Disclaimer

By using this material, you agree to abide by every local, state, and federal laws. You also agree that this material's author is free from liability of the consequences that may arise from any irresponsible action. Statements made and concepts conveyed throughout this product are personal opinions only. We do not warrant or represent that the use of the book will lead to any particular outcome or result. You are responsible for your behavior and conduct. None of the material contained herein is to be considered legal or personal advice.

Although the information contained in or made available through this product may be very useful and insightful, it cannot replace or substitute for the services of trained professionals in any field, including, but not limited to, psychological, financial, medical, or legal matters. Nor is anything in this book intended to be a diagnosis, prescription, recommendation, or cure for any specific kind of psychological, emotional, or sexual problem. If you think you may be suffering from any medical condition, you should seek immediate medical attention. You should never delay seeking medical advice, disregard medical advice, or discontinue medical treatment because of information in the book.

To put it simply, you alone are responsible for your behavior, so think about your actions thoroughly before doing them.

Table of Contents

Introduction

Before we start, I want you to understand one thing; only reading this book won't change anything. The ideas that I will present have the potential to improve the quality of your life significantly, if you allow them to, but you have to take action and apply the things you'll learn. When you have read this book and learned everything you need to know, you have to act upon it.

I have laid out the foundations and the essential fundamentals that will explain why and how to look at the world from a different point of view, but just reading this book once and then forgetting about it will lead you nowhere.

This book is not written as an analytical book or academic stuff to prove or disapprove any particular hypothesis or argument. It is prepared to act as a guide or a reference manual, which means that you have to act if you want to improve yourself because reading this book alone isn't going to magically enact any change.

It needs to be read several times to completely understand the concepts. It needs to be read 10 to 20 times as you strive to apply the principles contained herein, in your daily personal experiences for your improvement and realization of your potential. Take these principles to heart because each and every single one is important. None of these topics are fillers.

The main difference between men with happy and fulfilled lives and those with the opposite is the amount of work they put in. For the last time, you have to actively apply the knowledge learned from this book. If you combine the red pill knowledge with inaction and inactivity, the results could be disastrous. You have to absolutely own this material.

Lastly, my book focuses on bringing men up, not bringing women down. This book isn't coming from a place of hate, discrimination, or chauvinism. It comes from a place of understanding, accepting, and adapting. My goal in writing this book was to empower men, not undervalue women. The purpose of this book is to create more male leaders – God knows we need them now more than ever.

Part 1: Redefining The Red Pill

Regardless of what the media has told you, life gets better after the red pill. But it has to be the right kind of red pill, not the one that has been jammed down your throat by the media, men-hating feminists, and women-hating-emotionally-and-financially-hurt men. Let me redefine the red pill when it comes to dating.

"The Matrix is everywhere. It is all around us.
Even now, in this very room. You can see it when you look out your window
or when you turn on your television. You can feel it when you go to work...
When you go to church... When you pay your taxes. It is the world that has
been pulled over your eyes to blind you from the truth."
— Morpheus, The Matrix"

To get a better understanding of the red pill, let's dissect this quote. "The Matrix" and "the world" in this quote represent the ineffective and counterproductive (dating) strategies that have been "pulled over your eyes to blind you from the truth."

"The truth" represents effective and productive (dating) strategies that produce desired results and that only a handful of people are aware of. "The truth" is the existence of the Initial Physical Attraction and the Genuine Attraction scales. Something you will learn about in this book.

When I first started writing this book, I devoted a long chapter to defining the red pill. I soon realized I, like most men, began to accept other men's definition of and meaning to the red pill. Sadly, the red pill today stands for "living with reality in all its wretched horror." "The truth" has become some alternative, bitter and universal truth.

There are no general and universal truths; there are only different personal beliefs, which are nothing more than an interpretation of perception. In other words, the meaning we give to things, circumstances, and situations forms our realities.

There are, sadly, no such things as objective truths about women, money, fame, etc., no one-size-fits-all techniques or generalizations. There are only subjective, personal realities. It all depends on your perceptions. *"Taking the red pill"* means finding your own truth that works for you and produces the desired results, over and over again, just for you. Taking the red pill means you accept life for what it really is, not what you want it to be, and then do what you want with it, not what you are told.

Men who claim they will reveal the "truth" to you about women and women's "nature" are simply sharing their experiences from their own reality. Their ideologies, which are based on their personal experiences, and in most cases, terrible experiences, correlate the wrong causation as an explanation of their circumstances and outcomes. By using the wrong strategies to understand, attract, choose, and keep women, these men have become bitter and try to educate and "warn" other men. Their failing strategy didn't work, and they were not able to produce the desired outcome, and the only explanation is to blame women and their "nature." But, as we all know, correlation does not imply causation.

This has probably resulted in these men getting hurt—emotionally, financially, and spiritually. To make sense of it all, they look for answers outside of themselves, blaming female "nature" for their bad experiences because their egos won't allow them to look inside and search for answers and solutions. Gathering a crowd or a fanbase, where they can share a similar experience, creates a sense of belonging, which makes the pain manageable. I presume many of these men have good intentions, but I don't believe that this is what the red pill should be about. Instead of improving, most of these beliefs tend to hold us back, make us bitter and suspicious, believe me, I've been there.

I believe that taking the red pill means waking and opening up to the possibilities you haven't considered yet. It means to be more skeptical of your current, ineffective strategies and to consider that there could be different, deeper, and more effective beliefs, points of view, and strategies that aren't readily apparent to you. What you want to do is expose yourself to as much information as possible, and then take what applies to your life and your personal situation.

> *"Taking the red pill means you accept life for what it really is, not what you want it to be, and then do what you want with it, not what you are told."*
> — Stevan Terzić

I hope you are open to new ways of looking at things, trying new things out, and leaving your current, outdated, ineffective ways of thinking and your limiting beliefs, behind you. This will not be another book whining, complaining, and "exposing" female "nature" in order to make you feel accepted and comfortable for your inexperience and misgivings about human relationships.

On the contrary, this is a book that will hopefully push your boundaries, offer new ideas, and provide different strategies when it comes to dating and human relationships in general. This book is all about results, positive outcomes, and solutions.

"Don't make the mistake of waiting for a woman to start really living and enjoying your life."

—- Stevan Terzić

Part 2: Understanding Your World

"We are governed, our minds are molded, our tastes formed,
our ideas suggested, largely by men we have never heard of."
— Edward L. Bernays

Everything in the blue-pilled society boils down to one simple thing—control. Since our birth, we have been programmed to do what is expected from us. This programming starts with our parents, family, friends, school, television, internet, big companies, sitcoms, universities, advertisements, religions, and so forth. All different kinds of sources, which in some way are trying to control our thoughts, behaviors, the way we move, act and think.

This is also called social conditioning. It's the continuous practice of training people in general society to hold specific behaviors, beliefs, and desires that are "socially acceptable" or considered the norm.

A method usually employed in social conditioning is reinforcement, where certain behaviors are rewarded while the undesirable ones are punished. This is a classic form of conditioning, and it's even used in training lesser animals like dogs or lab rats.

The most widespread type of social conditioning, though, is the presentation of simple messages and images repeated over and over within very long periods until our minds assimilate them.

These messages can be conveyed explicitly, like a parent who teaches the things you should or shouldn't do. They can also be expressed implicitly, like romantic movies implying that if you're a nice enough guy who's persistent enough, you will eventually get the girl. The result of all this is a person who conforms to the right and wrong ideals of the society they live in.

Social conditioning has a lot of underlying issues, and somehow, all of them get swept under the rug without anyone noticing. It's not based on rationality, where people are influenced to adopt a certain behavior or belief based on logic or empirical evidence to support its "rightness."

The mechanisms of reward, punishment, and repetition are herding and indoctrinating people into having a specific aspect. This means that people can be trained into reacting a certain way, regardless if it's illogical, irrational, unethical, immoral, etc.

An even bigger issue that arises from social conditioning is that it's taking the lives of the general populace in the wrong direction. Whether deliberate or not, society is instilling the wrong values in us, unhealthy desires, fruitless behaviors, and inappropriate emotional reactions.

Just look at some health, lifestyle, and happiness statistical studies done in America. You will see how a large portion of our population is unhappy with the choices that they've made in life, the choices that were, apparently, ingrained in them to be the "right" choices.

Here are some statistics: It's estimated that 15% of the adult population will experience depression at some point in their lifetime[1], and 15.1% of U.S. adults smoke, which is down from 20.9% a decade earlier.[2]

---

[1] https://www.verywellmind.com/depression-statistics-everyone-should-know-4159056

[2] https://www.cdc.gov/tobacco/data_statistics/fact_sheets/adult_data/cig_smoking/

The beliefs, desires, emotional reactions, and behaviors that are considered the social norms are actually doing more harm than good. Here are some prime examples of the results of this almost inhumane social conditioning that affects every major aspect of our life:

Fitness, Health, and Wellness:

Despite being in a society that seemingly focuses on fitness and health, the fact of the matter is that the things we deem important are actually superficial. We care more about our looks than our actual health. As long as we *look* good, that's all that matters. People take part in unhealthy methods like extreme diets, steroids, surgery, toxic beauty products, and so on.

Most popular establishments focus on selling cheap but unhealthy food, and the food that we need to be healthy comes with inordinately high price tags. We are being taught to eat bad food as a normal way of living. We've never had more pills in human history, and yet we've never had more chronic disease.

Other examples of social conditioning regarding fitness, health, and wellness:

- Fasting is unhealthy.
- If you want a six-pack, you need to do 1000 crunches.
- Breakfast is the most important meal of the day.

Financial Success:

Society is forcing us to accept materialism and consumerism as ignorant individuals. Mass advertising is telling us to work 9 to 5 jobs to be able to buy the things we don't really need. There is no need to acquire more useless possessions to achieve higher status in society.

The fundamental mechanisms that drive our profit system are self-interest and self-preservation, which in turn cause all corporations and people to be corrupt, greedy, and to do whatever is necessary to continue profitability. Greed and fear of scarcity are created and amplified by the blue-pilled system that forces us to fight for our survival by competing for labor to acquire enough money to cover our costs of living. The monetary system is what makes our current society untrustworthy, egotistical, and self-orientated.

"A guy will come over to you and say, "I've got just the house you're looking for." He's a salesman. When a doctor says, 'I think your kidney has to come out,' I don't know if he's trying to pay off a yacht, or that my kidney has to come out- it's hard in the monetary system to trust people. If you came into my store and I said this lamp that I've got is pretty good, but the lamp in the next store is much better, I wouldn't be in business very long. It wouldn't work…
If I were ethical, it wouldn't work."
—Jacque Fresco, Zeitgeist: Addendum

Other examples of social conditioning regarding financial success:

- To succeed, you must destroy the competition.
- We see the failures of others as our success.
- Greed is encouraged and celebrated.
- A job means security.
- More money equals a happier life.

Love Life:

Society is promoting monogamy as the best type of romantic relationship, despite overwhelming evidence that supports otherwise. We are being stigmatized for having normal sexual desires and an appetite for sexual variety. How are we supposed to believe that having one family unit is desirable, even though hundreds of people are filing for divorce by the day?

Other examples of social conditioning regarding our love lives:

- Happy wife, happy life.
- Men need to kiss women's ass and solve their problems.
- Women fall in love with the Nice Guy.

Hollywood movies are another great example of terrible socialization that focuses on dating.

He gets the hot girl who, at the beginning of the movie, wasn't even interested in him. But, as long as he keeps pressing on, pushing, and proving his love, she eventually gives in.

Most popular sitcoms seem to feature a stupid, overweight oaf of a beta-husband, whose testicles are 100% owned by his confidant, assertive, attractive, calm, and sensible wife.

This sends the wrong message to every young boy watching:

- Their father needs to beg for boring starfish-sex.
- Their father always needs permission to go after his passions.
- Their father would collapse if his strong wife left him.

Young boys and men of the modern age are growing accustomed to this idea of attraction, seduction, romance, and love. For them, this is what is considered normal. These ineffective strategies can cause a lot of pain and suffering for otherwise good and genuinely nice men.

The Dangers Of Social Conditioning

We are supposed to believe that it is in our "nature" to blindly obey the authority without questioning it. It is not in our nature; human behavior appears to be environmentally determined. We are condoned and actively taught that we should obey people who deem legally based, morally right, or otherwise noteworthy.

The Milgram Experiment can help us understand how propaganda, social conditioning, and the right settings can get a moral person to do immoral acts.

In the early 1960s, a Yale University professor of psychology named Stanley Milgram carried out a famous study that had to do with psychological obedience. This study was done after the trial of a Nazi took place in Israel. The defense of the Nazis was that he merely followed the orders of his superiors. Milgram was interested to learn about the level at which obedience affects people's decision-making abilities. He and his team wanted to focus on people's obedience when it comes to authority.

They conducted an experiment where regular people were told to ask questions to a voluntary participant. Each time the participant answered a question incorrectly, they would receive an electric shock from a machine that was connected to them. The conductor served as the authoritarian of the experiment. The person administering the shocks did not know that this was an experiment and that the shocks were fake. But the volunteer participating in this experiment knew it was fake because he wasn't really getting shocked. He was merely an actor hired by the conductor and was told to act out the pain of the shocks as if they were real.

The conductor would ask the shock administrator to raise the voltage each time the participant answered a question incorrectly. In response, the participant would act out these terrifying screams of pain and suffering in front of everyone to make it look real.

Milgram wanted to see if the shock administrator would eventually disobey his commands and stop shocking the participant because of the supposed pain they were in. He was expecting the shock administrator would do that too. However, in every experiment they did, the shock administrator kept listening to the conductor and continued to shock the participant on command. The morality of the situation was not enough to get the shock-administrator to disobey their authority figure.

In conclusion, the results of these psychological experiments are rather scary. They show that most people are willing to obey someone else just because they are wearing a white coat, a laboratory coat, or merely act authoritatively. Morality appears to have no, or minimal bearing when authoritarians are in the picture. It has to power to unconsciously make us think we are doing the right thing, even if we are physically hurting others. That's how powerful social conditioning can be.

If executed correctly, social conditioning can instill all sorts of limiting beliefs in people, making them unable to realize, let alone reach their full potential.

Social conformity

There are things in life that define the existence of the plugged-in people— social conformity. This type of social influence is the number one cause that hampers personal progress and stays in the way of people's fulfillment and happiness.

Social conformity is a type of social influence that results in a change of habits, behavior, or belief to fit in or go along with a group of people around you—changing your opinion and views when in the minority or following traditions you don't like or agree with, are just a few examples of social conformity.

People who do not conform to their peer group are considered nonconformist, eccentric, maverick, individualist, exception, outsider, or misfit. They are less liked, accepted, and even punished by the group. If mentally weak, these people can become outcasts.

Social conformity has been well researched and documented. A great example would be The Asch Conformity Experiments.

In the early 1950s, the Asch conformity experiments took place to see if humans naturally agree with big groups of people even when they know it is wrong to do so. The tests were conducted on a single person at a time by putting him/her in a room which contained several other people. These people served as the actors of the experiment. The conductor showed the actors and the subject a piece of paper that contained three lines of different sizes on it.

He asked the actors to state which line on the paper was the longest. On purpose, the actors chose the wrong line in order to see whether the subjects would disagree, using their own logic or go with everyone else's answers, simply because there is strength in numbers.

Of course, the subjects did not know these people were testing them. They thought those were the answers they meant to give. So, the subjects had to either conform and agree with everyone's answer or choose to disagree and feel the pressure of being the minority opinion.

The results of the study showed that humans would rather agree and conform to the majority of people to avoid being criticized or ridiculed, even if they, with absolute certainty, know what they are doing is wrong.

*"People will do more to avoid
pain than they will do to gain pleasure."*
— Tony Robbins

Although some social conditioning can't be avoided unless you go live alone in the woods, but I assume that's not something you want. It is essential to acknowledge that conformity isn't necessarily always a bad thing. At the end of the day, we are social animals. We feel safe, comfortable, and content when we are accepted by, when we fit in and when we belong to a particular group. From time to time, we all feel the need to relate to and connect with someone. This is normal and absolutely essential for a happy and healthy mind. Love and connection are one of our six core needs, after all.

Social conformity becomes a problem when our true desires and thoughts **must be suppressed to conform the society in order to avoid being criticized or ridiculed.** It becomes a problem when we must go out of our way to conform and meet societal expectations.

If you want to do something that might be considered outside the norm, don't let that, or anything for that matter, stop you from doing it.

You only need to follow these two rules:
1) Just like Arnold Schwarzenegger said, **"Break the rules, not the law."**
2) It goes without saying; **you cannot harm other animals or human beings in any way.** Neither physically, emotionally, nor spiritually.

It is important to be able to identify any kind of social conditioning that may be negatively influencing you. This way, you can counteract them.

1. **Don't ever assume that you're immune from social conditioning.**

Many make the mistake of thinking that they're so smart that any negative forms of social conditioning don't affect them, and that false societal ideas or behaviors have never influenced them.

Based on experience, this is impossible. Assuming that you're above any form of social conditioning simply means that you're the biggest slave of it. Society has lambasted us with thousands of propaganda from our youth to up to our adulthood, and it's almost impossible to completely escape from. It's best to know your enemy and acknowledge their power, rather than let yourself be consumed by your own arrogance.

2. **Question your current value system.**

Observe yourself for any recurring behaviors, ideas, emotions, and desires. It's impossible to be aware of everything you think, feel, or do. What you can do is try to observe any recurring patterns that impact your life significantly.

To start, you can practice being conscious of your thoughts, actions, behaviors, and feelings in a variety of situations. If you've discovered something that you've consistently believed to be true, question its validity. If you notice something that you've habitually been doing, ask yourself if this behavior has any real use. Question everything and judge them based on their usefulness. Why do you do certain things? How did you started doing it, and when? Who told you to think like that?

This is an excellent method of pinpointing any implanted counterproductive belief systems and behaviors, feelings, and desires. If you think that any of these elements can be commonly found in most individuals or if you feel that large societal groups promote them, then they're most likely an effect of social conditioning.

Make a habit of this self-examination process. Be rational with your observations and judgments. It might be difficult at first, but with time, it will get easier. We will talk about this in the following chapters.

3. Heed the advice of experts.

In every field, there will always be experts who can offer real knowledge. These individuals have years of experience and expertise under their belt. They are well versed in many types of research regarding their area of expertise, and odds are, might have performed a few themselves. They also know how to back up their claims with empirical evidence instead of hearsay.

More often than not, the ideas of these people are infinitesimally different from the mainstream media's or society's. And without fail, their ideas are usually the ones that make more sense. Unfortunately, ideas that don't fit into a specific agenda, even if they are better, are often shoved under the rug and kept hidden from the public.

Take advantage of these people's expertise and learn from their pools of knowledge. Read their books, take up the courses they offer, and go to their events. Study every subject under the sun, but focus on politics, history, psychology, social science, economy, and health.

Knowledge is power. It's the only thing that can reveal the truth about social conditioning, the blue-pill world, and help you find the right path.

4. Get out of your comfort zone.

As humans, we tend to interact with people who are similarly built from us, people with the same opinions, thoughts, and ideas. We surround ourselves with people who want the same things, dislike the same things, and behave the same way as us.

This desire to be with like-minded individuals is entirely natural, understandable, and even useful at times. But limit the times you do so because it's also good to step out of your comfort zone. Meet other kinds of people and learn about their point of view and where they are coming from.

Often, this confirms your behaviors and beliefs, but there are moments where you will realize that you're in the wrong, all because of bad social conditioning. Think of this as pulling the wool out of your eyes and see the world in a different light.

"Every society honors its living conformists and its dead troublemakers."
— Marshall McLuhan

"Those who do not move, do not notice their chains."
— Rosa Luxemburg

The five key fundamentals of this chapter::

- Don't ever assume that you're immune from social conditioning.
- Question your current value system.
- Heed the advice of experts.
- Get out of your comfort zone.

Part 3: Understanding Women and Attraction

Before we start, I would like you to know how and why I define certain words in this book.

Let's start with the words "female" and "woman." A woman is, by my definition, a sexually attractive, feminine female. In order to call a female a woman, she must have biological value. So, when I talk about "women," visualize a sexually attractive, feminine female, whatever that might entail for you. When I say "a female," imagine a sexually unattractive female, depending on what that means for you.

I deliberately choose to use the word women's *behavior* and not women's *nature*. Human behavior appears to be environmentally determined. This means that if the Sentinelese tribe—possibly the most isolated tribe in the world—raised you and you'd never seen any other people or cultures, you'd adopt their value systems and their ways of thinking about, looking at, and explaining the various aspects of the world.

This principle applies to all of us, men and women. All behavior is learned; there is no original human nature. Women are not born liars, cheaters, manipulators, gold diggers, and so on. They picked that up from their environment, i.e., our society. It is easy to blame human "nature" for your problems and disagreements—people who use the word "nature" or "instinct" to explain actions only do so because they can't account for human behavior. Regardless of what you believe, whether human "nature" is learned or not, you now understand why I don't use the word nature to explain women's behavior.

You should know by now that women are a lot more emotional than men, far more dynamic and ever-changing human beings. You might have understood this from reading books, forums, or—

possibly—from your own experiences. To attract women, you need to know, understand, and accept their behavior. Once you do this, you can start focusing on seducing them, rather than envying them, having arguments with them, chasing them, spending money on them, or applying other useless and ineffective dating strategies.

In order to truly understand and accept women's behavior, we have to know and understand what drives us, males and females, to act the way that we do. How do we measure our feeling of self-worth? What is beneath everything we feel, and how does that help us assess the quality of our lives? If you find yourself asking these questions, the answer lies in knowing the basic things that we all need as human beings.

We are taught from childhood that everyone is unique, and every person is shaped by his or her exclusive experiences. While that is true, there are some things that link us together and make us similar. In his book *How To Live 365 Days a Year*, Dr. John Schindler pointed out that every human being has six basic needs: Love, Security, Creative Expression, Recognition, New Experiences, and Self-Esteem.

Basically, the list is a variation on Abraham Maslow's famous Hierarchy of Needs, which was introduced in the early 1940s. Similarly, in her book *Relationship Breakthrough*, Chloé Madanes recognizes the importance of Maslow's Hierarchy of Needs and combines these insights with those of John A. Schindler. She lists the following six basic needs: Certainty/Comfort, Uncertainty/Variety, Significance, Love/Connection, Growth, and Contribution.

These needs directly affect how we go about our lives, and each person prioritizes these needs distinctively. That is why our lives play out in different trajectories, and we go on to fulfill individually drawn destinies.

Changing the language somewhat, here is my interpretation of these six human needs.

1. **Certainty/Comfort/Control:** the need to feel in control, feel secure, and comfortable. The need and assurance you can avoid pain or minimize the stress of uncertainty and gain or create pleasure.

2. **Uncertainty/Variety/Thrill/Excitement/New Experiences:** the need for a change to relieve boredom, predictability, and stagnation.

3. **Significance/Recognition/Validation:** the need to gain a sense of significance and importance of others. Feeling unique, wanted, meaningful, important, relevant, and needed.

4. **Connection/Love:** the need to love, be loved, and to belong. The need to make deep connections with people. The need to feel close to someone or something.

5. **Growth/Advancement:** the need to grow intellectually emotionally, spiritually. The need to learn and evolve. An expansion of capacity, capability or understanding

6. **Contribution/Giving back:** the need to contribute to something greater than yourself. The need for adding value. A sense of service and focus on helping, giving to, and supporting others.

How we behave depends on whether or not our needs are being met. Most people have one or two needs that drive 80% of their behaviors. It is our personality that dictates what needs we prioritize over the others. It is extremely likely that you are trying to meet one or two of your most prioritized needs at any given time. If you are having a tough time doing so, this is going to negatively impact how you feel about yourself.

These six human needs influence your deepest motivations. They also determine how you go about prioritizing your decisions and actions throughout your whole life. Well, the same applies to every other human being, including women. They are, just like everyone else, fundamentally driven by the desire to fulfill their six core human needs, especially the first four because they are essential for human survival. The last two needs, Growth and Contribution, are required for human actualization/fulfillment. Once you grasp and fully understand this concept of six basic human needs, everything everybody does will make a lot more sense.

Redefining Hypergamy

Hypergamy is a women's reproductive strategy. It's women's search for a man who can provide her with healthy genes and, at the same time, offer the best provisioning, long-term security, safety, and parental investment. In other words, they are looking for someone who can, indirectly, meet two or more of their six human needs.

Beta males can often provide women with only long-term benefits and security, thus fulfilling only one women's need; the need for certainty.

Now, if a woman would have only one need, the need for certainty, beta males, with a stable job and no mystery about them, wouldn't have any problem getting and keeping women. But because all females, just like all males, are fundamentally driven by the desire to fulfill all, and not just one of their six core needs, the beta male inevitably fails.

It's not that women want a high-status male solely for his high status or his resources; it is because they believe that these men could meet two or more of their six core human needs. And in most cases, these men can do just that. But in some cases, being wealthy and having resources doesn't necessarily make you resourceful. What I mean by that is having the ability to obtain resources and reach high status doesn't automatically translate into having the ability or knowledge on how to meet two or more of the women's core human needs. That's why you hear about wealthy men getting cheated on with a hot pool boy. Sadly, most men assume this correlation implies causation.

There are different ways of meeting those needs; some are more effective and sustainable than others. The key is to find out which of the six core needs are her primary ones, and how to meet them effectively. All women have prioritized different core needs, but there is some generalization to be made, which I've no doubt you can see and understand from the following explanation.

When it comes to younger women, ages from 18 up to 25 years, the need for uncertainty will be the driving force in her love and sex life. When a woman reaches the age of 25 and up, the more they start to value the need for certainty. Note: this is a rough estimate and highly dependable on the women's current situation, her past experience, standards, and values. Because women have a shorter reproductive timespan than men, time is of the essence. This is also the reason why women appear ruthless and heartless when it comes to dumping men who don't have a clue about how to meet women's core needs.

Attraction

On the internet, you can find a lot of guides that can supposedly teach you how to attract ANY girl in the world. Don't be so gullible because this is far from the truth. That's the type of bullshit that blue-pilled beta males love to believe.

You cannot get ANY woman you want. Sure, you can approach any woman you want, but you will only waste your time, money, and energy. Why? Think about it this way — can ANY female get you in bed? Of course not, because you don't find every female attractive. You have most likely ranked them or put them on a 1 to 10 scale, or something similar. I like to call that scale *the Initial Physical Attraction.*

Physically Attraction

To have a chance with a woman, she must be Initially Physically Attracted to you on a scale of 5.0 or above. Anything lower than that, and it will not be worth your effort. The benefit you'll gain will be significantly outweighed by what you'd have to put up with. So, when a woman's **Initial Physical Attraction** to you is 4.9 or lower, you must treat her as if she is not attracted to you at all (or she is **Inauthentically Attracted** to you - more on this later.)

I can sense you are getting confused about these terms, so let me clear things up. Why do I call it Initial Physical Attraction and not a level of interest? Because the level of interest means nothing when it comes to dating. You don't want merely **interest**, because all kinds of people can be interested in you, and that's great, but that's not what you are looking for. What you want is a pure **physical attraction.** It doesn't have to be much, 5.0 at a bare minimum, but it has to be present. You want to spend your time, energy, and money only on women who are **Initially Physically Attracted** to you.

The Initial Physical Attraction is based on your physical appearance. Scoring 5.0 or higher means you've passed her physical attraction test. Physical attraction is based on visually apparent factors, like your hair, clothing, body language, figure, etc.

Every woman has a different idea of what she finds physically attractive. For some women, you will score a 9.3 on the Initial Physical Attraction scale, while for other women, you'll barely make to 3.8. Physical attraction is not a logical decision or a choice. People don't choose who they are attracted to. It is what it is. There is not much you can do about it, except always make sure to look your best. And by best, I mean clean, healthy, and energized.

After the Initial Physical Attraction comes **Genuine Attraction**, the same scale of 1 to 10 applies. The difference between these two is that you have very little control over Initial Physical Attraction, but you have almost full control when it comes to Genuine Attraction.

Genuine Attraction is based on emotions and feelings. It's all about how you make her feel. The better you are at meeting her needs, the higher you score on her Genuine Attraction scale. In essence, it all boils down to meeting two or more of her six core human needs.

These two scales are correlated with each other. Let me give you an example: the lower you score on her Initial Physical Attraction scale, the looks department, the higher you **must** score on her Genuine Attraction scale (feelings and emotions).

The higher you score on her Initial Physical Attraction scale, the lower you can score on the Genuine Attraction scale. But on both scales, you must score 5.0 or higher.

That is why really handsome and genetically blessed fellas can get away with more screw-ups than an average-looking guy. But again, only to a certain degree. When they drop below 5.0 on her Genuine Attraction scale, no matter how hot they are, they are out! This is what's happening in Hollywood all the time. Celebrity divorce rates are so high because male celebrities, who score high on the Initial Physical Attraction, don't know how to either maintain Genuine Attraction or don't know how to raise it.

That's why they also tend to make the same mistake in their second, third, or even fourth marriage.

Inauthentic Attraction

Inauthentic Attraction occurs when a woman acts as if she has Initial Physical Attraction for you, but in reality, she is only attracted to the things you can do for her. Thus, this attraction is based on hidden motives and is, therefore, inauthentic. Unlike physical attraction, Inauthentic Attraction **is** a logical decision. Inauthentic Attraction can also be lowered or raised based on your behavior.

Inauthentic Attraction occurs when a manipulative, needy, and dependent woman has below 5.0 Initial Physical Attraction for you. It is so low that you are probably not even a blip on her radar. The thought of you sleeping with her hasn't even crossed her mind. You just simply don't make her vagina tingle. But because she is manipulative, needy, selfish, and hasn't been able to find any better and healthier ways of meeting her core needs, she will make a logical decision and choose to be inauthentically attracted to you.

A good, healthy woman with the right attitude, who has a below 5.0 Initial Physical Attraction for you, will not make the logical decision and choose to be inauthentically attracted to you. She might find it difficult to say no to you or reject you directly, but she won't purposefully misuse your resources, time, and energy for her selfish reasons.

That's why I make a distinction between the Inauthentic Attraction and low Initial Physical Attraction because some men could interpret the latter as just that, low physical attraction. They would rationalize and say things like, "*So, she is physically attracted to me, but her attraction for me is just very low. And if it's low, I can raise it by buying her x or taking her to an expensive restaurant.*"

You cannot, nor should you ever try to convert Inauthentic Attraction into something authentic. You will always end up disappointed, emotionally exhausted, with fewer resources, cheated on, and, most importantly, you will lose time you can never get back.

Gold Diggers

All women can fake Initial Physical Attraction, but none can fake Genuine Attraction, hence the term "Genuine Attraction." There is an easy test you can do early on to find out if a woman is Inauthentically Attracted to you or not. Cheap dates. Women who are Inauthentically Attracted to you will not go out if you take them to a coffee or fun activity date for four dates straight. They might put up with it for two dates, but they will continuously ask you or strongly hint at when are you going to take them to that expensive restaurant. It should be clear she is only looking for someone to pay for her dinner, a fancy, expensive dinner.

Delete her number as soon as she asks you these types of questions. You don't want to spend any of your time and effort on these kinds of gold diggers. You want a woman who is Genuinely Attracted to you, someone who values and appreciates how you make her feel, not someone whose feelings you can buy or negotiate. The dating game for men has become brutal, so in order to win, you have to become brutal as well. When it comes to a gold digger, you have to adopt a zero-tolerance policy.

Attention Whore & Time Wasters

Another type of woman who often chooses to get Inauthentically Attracted to men is the Attention Whore. These women will act as if they are Initially Physically Attracted to you, but in truth, all they want is to make sure you are physically attracted to them. Once they get your validation, you will become another notch on her belt. Another guy who is drooling all over her. Another guy who is meeting her need for certainty. Which is nice, but it does not create attraction.

Some indicators of an Attention Whore:

- She will never find time to date you. She will always come up with all kinds of excuses.
- She will never give you the exact time when to call, pick her up, etc.
- She only wants to go on a date if it's favorable to her, like group dates and very crowded places. You're not likely to get her isolated.
- She loves to set "maybe" dates.
- She doesn't bother to fill out her online dating profile; instead, she just asks you to follow her on social media.

All of these indicate she isn't physically attracted to you at all. All she wants is your attention. That's why she is vague about time, meeting up, setting up the dates, etc. These women will be as ambiguous as they can be. They will never confirm a specific date or ask to reschedule. Why? Because they don't want to see you. These women love to set a "maybe" date.

Never accept a "maybe" date. By accepting a "maybe" date, you're essentially sending a message saying that it's ok to disrespect you and waste your time. Accepting a "maybe" date is approval-seeking behavior. A man who knows what he wants sticks to a rigid timetable. That is the only way to get the upper hand and not take the bait, is never to accept a "maybe" date. Say something like, "It's ok, let's make it another night when your schedule is tighter. Have a good night."

After that, delete her number. Why delete her number, you ask? Why would you keep it? You basically told her to contact you if she wants to schedule a new date. Under no circumstances will you ever contact this woman again. If she has high Genuine Attraction for you, she will initiate contact, and if not, you'll never hear from this woman back again. Good! You calling/texting her and asking her out again, will not raise her Genuine Attraction for you—she will just lose all respect for you.

Women who have a high-Interest level set definite dates – with no underlying reason other than to see you again. If not, always play the role of a gentleman, and never openly accuse her of wasting your time. It won't raise her Initial Physical Attraction or her Genuine Attraction for you.

Just smile, say goodbye, and remember to delete her number.

Indicators Of Attraction

Initial Physical Attraction

Initial Physical Attraction can be summarized in one word; effortless. Everything should go smoothly. There would be very little to no resistance from the woman. The higher her Initial Physical Attraction, the less resistance you will encounter. The closer you are to 5.0, the more barriers will stand in your way.

When a woman has high Initial Physical Attraction for you, she won't hesitate to give you her number. Heck, if it's really high, she might ask you for your number.

Some indicators of **high** Initial Physical Attraction of a flexible woman with a good attitude are:

- She can't keep a smile off her face while in your presence. (5.5)
- She holds prolonged eye contact. (5.8)
- She plays with her hair while in your presence. (6.1)
- She smiles at you. (6.5)

- She enters your personal space. (7.2)
- She initiates physical contact. (8)
- She tries to keep the conversation going by asking you fun and quality questions. (8.5)
- She gives you her phone number with no resistance or hesitation at all. (9)
- She gives you her phone number without you ask her for it. (10)

As a healthy man, you'll only spend your precious time and effort on women that are 5.0 or higher on **your** scale of Initial Physical Attraction, meaning she has to pass **your** physical attraction test. But as a red-pilled alpha male, **you'll also keep in mind how these women perceive you**. It's highly unlikely you will ever raise her Genuine Attraction for you if her Initial Physical Attraction was 4.7 or lower, so it's pointless to waste your time, energy, and money on these types of women. The benefit you'll gain is significantly outweighed by what you'd have to put up with. Remember that sentence.

Some indicator of **low** Initial Physical Attraction of a flexible woman with a good attitude are:

- She doesn't make any effort to check you out. (4.9)
- She doesn't hold eye contact or smiles at you. (4.6)
- She acts cold or distant. (4.3)
- She doesn't put any effort into keeping the conversation going. (3.8)
- She avoids asking and answering questions. (3.7)
- She acts shocked and confused when you ask for her phone number. (3.0)
- She doesn't want to give you her phone number. (2.0)
- She screams and runs away when you approach her. (1.0)

To her, your Initial Physical Attraction for her is irrelevant. Women do not care how much you're physically or genuinely attracted to them. If they did, nice guys would be getting laid left and right. But this isn't the case. This is why it's essential to realize that if you score 4.9 or lower on a woman's Initial Physical Attraction scale, it does not matter how much **you** are Initially Physically Attracted to them. **The only thing that matters is how physically attracted a woman is to you.**

The same applies when it comes to Genuine Attraction; it is irrelevant how much you're Genuinely Attracted to her.

"The only thing that matters is how Genuinely Attracted SHE is, to you; how positively you are affecting her feelings."

And if you are not able to pass her physical attraction test (Initial Physical Attraction lower than 5.0) and meet her core needs (Genuine Attraction lower than 5.0), there is nothing you can say, do or give her to increase her attraction for you. No stuffed animal, a giant heart-shaped balloon, expensive dinner, or a romantic poem will do the trick. The Initial Physical Attraction and Genuine Attraction aren't a choice. We can choose as to whether we want to date someone, but there is either inherent chemistry or there isn't.

Naturally, negotiation doesn't work on chemical processes. Initial Physical Attraction and Genuine Attraction are both results of complex chemical processes, and that's why **they can't be negotiated.** Unfortunately, this doesn't stop blue-pilled men from trying.

Genuine Attraction

When it comes to the game of dating, there is nothing more important than knowing how to spot a woman who has a **low** Genuine Attraction for you. A typical blue-pilled man deludes himself into believing that the woman he has a high Genuine Attraction for, must feel the same way about him. This is the biggest mistake men today make. And because of it, these men waste a lot of time, energy, and money on women who simply don't have 5,0, or higher Genuine Attraction for them. The problem is the man's ego.

Ego

Our ego is the driving force that pushes us to work harder and never give up, regardless of the situation. Whether it's looking for the right line of work, achieving goals, making tough decisions on the spot, getting in better shape, or even loftier goals like helping out humanity, our ego is always the catalyst. Our ego pushes us forward and gives us an unusual amount of determination and perseverance.

The same can't be said when love and sexual attraction are brought to the table. In these cases, your ego is a vulnerability, a curse, even.

Where love is concerned, a man's ego:

- Blinds him from a woman's bad behavior.
- Rationalizes said behavior.
- Ignores the red flags.
- Exaggerates a woman's Genuine Attraction for him.
- Disengages him from reality by overlooking negative outcomes.

When in the process of gauging her Genuine Attraction level, put your ego to the side. Look the things objectively and don't allow emotions to make the decisions for you.

Let's assume you have passed the Initial Physical Attraction test and got her phone number. Now it's time to put your ego to the side, gauge, and raise her Genuine Attraction for you.

Some indicator of **high** Genuine Attraction of a flexible woman with a good attitude are:

- She acts excited when you call her. (5.5)
- She asks fun and engaging questions during your short conversation on the phone. (5.8)
- She is flexible when you are picking a date to see each other. (6.3)
- She is on time on the day of the date. (6.5)
- She laughs at your corny joke. (6.8)
- She is fun, playful, and teases you back during the date. (7.2)
- She intentionally touches you on the leg, arm, chest, or shoulder. (8.4)
- She opens up and willing to talk about personal things. (8.5)
- She gazes into your eyes, stands extremely close to you, and touches you. (8.7)
- She **initiates** kissing. (8.9)
- She suggests you two go to her or your place. (9.5)
- She **initiates** passionate sex. (9.7)

As you can see, the higher her Genuine Attraction, the more easy-going she will be. It's effortless being with these kinds of women. Everything should run smoothly. That's what you want.

When things are effortless, life is good. But when her Genuine Attraction for you is on the low side, closer to 5.0, the more barriers you will encounter.

Some indicator of **low** Genuine Attraction of a flexible woman with a good attitude are:

- She isn't as flexible while arranging a date. Even if you've passed the Initial Physical Attraction test, calling too soon could be the reason her Genuine Attraction for you plummets. (5.3)
- She wants you to confirm the date. (5.1)
- She isn't communicating or being open. (5.1)
- She starts to nag, complains, and puts you down. (5.2)
- She avoids making sexual advances. Doesn't initiate touching, kissing, etc.(5.02)
- She rejects your sexual advances. (5.01)

If her Genuine Attraction drops below 5.0, it is over. Women rarely, if ever, give second chances in life. You get a lot of shots to raise her attraction as long as it stays above 5.0. If it drops below that, forget about it. Again, the benefit you'll gain is significantly outweighed by what you'd have to put up with – it's not worth it.

Certainty & Uncertainty

Genuine Attraction is anything but stable. Based on your behavior, it fluctuates. To keep it elevated or even raise it, you need to continually meet two or more of her core needs, especially the need for uncertainty, thrill, and excitement. And that is the key to keeping women genuinely interested and sexually attracted.

The need for uncertainty is what keeps her wondering and makes you a challenge in her eyes, but even more importantly, bored (read "certainty") is the killer of sexual attraction.

Women are bombarded with nice guys who are just waiting to fulfill their, probably already met, need for certainty. These men are, therefore, highly predictable, boring, and mean anything but uncertainty, thrill, and excitement. That's why women crave men who can meet their need for uncertainty and can offer some excitement in their lives. These men are scarce and, therefore, highly valuable to and wanted by feminine women.

A lot of books teach you how to be a challenge for a woman. Although the outcomes are similar, the method is profoundly different. Being a challenge is prone to subjectivity because its purpose is to measure responses that cannot always be quantified. What you believe "being a challenge" means, might not be considered a challenge by the woman you are dating. Always trying to be a challenge for her could be regarded as pleasing behavior. It gets tiresome after a while. You may start to feel like you are always doing things to be a challenge. By looking at it from a different angle, an angle where you just make the woman feel uncertain and unsure about where she stands with you, you feel like a weight is immediately lifted from your shoulders.

Making someone feel uncertain about where they stand with you is much easier. It not needy, it's quite the opposite. Uncertainty is less subjective; we all inherently know how to make someone feel uncertain and unsure about where they stand with us. It might sound harsh, but remember, feeling uncertainty and excitement is one of our core human needs. You are doing women a huge favor by meeting their need for uncertainty. If you believe this is immoral, I've got some bad news for you; have a nice life being a nice guy.

Meeting Her Need For Uncertainty

So, how does one go about meeting the women's need for uncertainty? It is easier than you think. Think of everything that would make you uncertain about someone, and then do just that to her. Ask yourself if the things you are doing now would make her sure or unsure about you? If you are to text her back right now, would that make her certain or uncertain about where she stands with you? What about if you waited till tomorrow to text her back? Would that make her more certain or uncertain about you? How about if you plan fun dates but avoid mentioning anything about getting serious or really anything about the future? And what about if you don't answer the phone over the weekend? You get the point. *I will lay down some "rules" for you that will guarantee you can meet her need for uncertainty in the following chapters.*

Beta males can't meet women's need for uncertainty because they, themselves, struggle with it. They can't handle uncertainty; they want and need to know where they stand with a woman. That's why they make fatal mistakes, and even though the women may have had Initial Physical Attraction for them, they are unwillingly lowering Genuine Attraction by continually, and unknowingly, meeting the women's need for certainty by asking questions that offer them assurance about where they stand with them.

The need for certainty and uncertainty are negatively correlated to each other. When one increases, the other decreases, and vice versa. The key is to prolong meeting and fulfilling both of them for as long as possible, all the while the woman remains to crave either one or the other. This will increase the satisfaction when one of her needs is being fulfilled by you, which in turn will make her crave it more when it's not.

From a woman's point of view, what does it look like when a man always responds to her text as soon as he gets them? She knows where she stands with him. What does it look like when a man asks her for a relationship? She knows where she stands with him. What does it look like when a man is willing to put his purpose aside to be with her? She knows where she stands with him. You get the point. They all meet her need for certainty and assurance.

Every action a beta male takes is unconsciously meeting her need for certainty on some level. In fact, beta males avoid uncertainty and do their best to assure women where she stands with them—a completely counterproductive method to raise a woman's Genuine Attraction.

The other extreme is typical bad boys. Although extremely effective in fulfilling a woman's need for uncertainty, these men don't have a clue how to fulfill a woman's need for certainty. That's why most relationships with bad boys are incredibly passionate yet highly unsustainable. Most relationships with bad boys don't last a very long time, that is unless the bad boy abandons their turbulent lifestyle for a more stable and predictable life. As discussed earlier, the older women get, the more they start to value their need for certainty. That's why typical bad boys are found highly attractive and wanted by relatively younger women but tend to be viewed as childish by more mature women.

Although the older a woman gets, the more she starts to value her need for certainty, her need for the thrill, excitement, and uncertainty will always remain there for you or other men to fulfill. The ways you, or other men, go about fulfilling that need will and must change with time and maturity.

Meeting Both of Her Needs

A red-pilled alpha male can meet the women's need for uncertainty and knows when to satisfy her need for certainty. As mentioned earlier, the need for certainty and uncertainty are negatively correlated to each other. Both needs must be met.

When it comes to dating, you can meet her need for certainty by asking for her phone number, setting up dates, having fun on those dates, laughing, etc. All are indicators that you like her; it makes her feel certain about you and where she stands with you. This is all you need to do to meet her need for certainty, especially in the beginning.

When it comes to dating, you can meet her need for uncertainty by not chitchatting on the phone, meeting her once per week, never talking about the future, not coming on too strong too quickly, not rushing to get her into bed, etc. All are indicators that you might not like her that much: it makes her feel uncertain about you and where she stands with you.

This uncertainty is what creates sexual tension and genuine attraction. Women crave both uncertainty and certainty from men. But uncertainty, thrill, and excitement make them feel young, stimulated, and alive; a rare and addictive feeling that creates a dopamine rush, always leaving them wanting for more. You are doing them a disservice by not meeting their need for uncertainty.

Getting Serious

When you have been continually and successfully meeting a woman's need for uncertainty for long periods, how long depends on the woman, all you need to do is wait on her to tell when she is ready for you to fulfill her need for certainty. Because the two needs are negatively correlated to each other, when one overflows, the other one drains out and needs to get filled up.

When a woman wants you to fulfill her need for certainty, she will ask you for it. She might express it by wanting to see you more often, or on the weekends. She might ask you if you could get together on a Friday or a Saturday night. (Assuming you gave the impression that you always had something better to do those nights.)

Questions like where your fun and sexual relationship is headed might hint that she is willing to get a bit more serious with you or even get married. (Depending on how long you two have been dating.) You need to explore these questions with her by making her explicitly tell you what her desires are.

Ask her question, "What do you mean by x?" You want to get her to explicitly tell you what she wants. Whatever that might be, spending more time together, getting into a serious monogamous relationship, or even getting married, you ultimately get to decide where you are going with this woman. Alphas have the choice, and betas don't.

Actions Versus Words

It is believed that women use an average of 20,000 words per day, nearly three times the mere 7,000 spoken by men. Men are pretty blunt and overt with their feelings, and this manifests in the way they communicate. Men are all about instructions, step-by-step manuals, solving problems, and reaching satisfying solutions. We, men, like the "simpler" style of communication. We like to keep it short and direct. Women, on the other hand, are more covert when it comes to communication and expression of their feelings, wants, and desires.

They prefer to use covert communication because they don't want to hurt the feelings of other people; they try to avoid confrontation (mainly with angry and crazy men) and direct rejecting someone. They don't like to be cornered.

What does covert communication look like? It's not apparent, very roundabout, using gestures and looks with hidden meanings instead of direct communication. It's basically being and acting very passive.

Have you ever had a girl tell you she wants to go out with you, but somehow something always comes up? Have you ever had a girl tell you how sweet and friendly you are, and she would be happy if she only could find a nice man like you?

Men get frustrated when they "just don't get" how women communicate and say one thing but do the other. Being merely aware of this simple fact can drastically improve your quality of life when it comes to interacting and understanding women. The solution: knowing that women communicate on a covert level when it comes to the big picture stuff, you shouldn't listen to what a woman says, instead look at her action. Her actions will tell you everything you need to know.

If she says she wants to see you, but somehow something always comes up, it means she doesn't want to see you. There is no need to ask her again. Genuine Attraction is expressed through actions, not words. A woman might say how much she likes you, but if her actions tell you otherwise, you have to base your conclusion on those actions.

Most females assume men communicate the same way they do. They pay close attention to our actions, movements, body language, voice tonality, and pitch, especially in the beginning, while in the process of getting to know us. For example, if you send her a text saying you miss her, but you do it on a Saturday night, it tells her you are a loser with no friends. Why would you otherwise have time to send a text on a Saturday night? It's not what you say; it's how you say it and, in this case, when. Actions speak louder than words.

Women with no integrity don't mean what they say and say what they mean. "My dog is sick, sorry!" doesn't mean, "My dog is really sick, but when my dog is feeling better, we should totally get together!" Women without integrity aren't raised with typical masculine virtues like loyally, courage, respect, honor, and prudence. Don't expect them to have these virtues, and don't waste your time explaining these virtues to women raised without integrity.

The five key fundamentals of this chapter:

- Meet women's need for uncertainty, thrill, and excitement. Meeting her need for uncertainty is what creates sexual attraction and tension.

- You must score 5,0 or higher on her Initial Physical Attraction scale in order to climb on her Genuine Attraction scale.

- Initial Physical Attraction can be faked by Gold Diggers, Attention Whores, and Time Wasters.

- Be honest with your situation; put your ego aside. Gauge her Genuine Attraction by her actions and be brutal when it comes to making a decision whether to continue putting more energy into her or move on to the next.

- Let her initiate the relationship/marriage talk; it must be her idea.

"The better you are at making excuses, the more your life will suck."

— Stevan Terzić

Part 4: The Approach, First Dates, and Red Flags

Choosing Signals

Choosing signals are those subtle ways women signal romantic interest. It basically all boils down to this: she makes it easy for you to approach. Choosing signals means a woman has High Initial Physical Attraction for you. But there is a caveat, to which I will return.

We have discussed some indicators of high Initial Physical Attraction of a flexible woman with a good attitude, but for the sake of convenience, I'll list them again.

- She can't keep a smile off her face while in your presence. (5.5)
- She holds prolonged eye contact. (5.8)
- She plays with her hair while in your presence. (6.1)
- She smiles at you. (6.5)
- She enters your personal space. (7.2)
- She initiates physical contact. (8)

Do not try to memorize these because doing so tends to make your interactions awkward. Instead, try to ingrain them with your instincts by developing situational awareness. If anything, if you notice a girl smiling and maintaining eye contact with you and/or standing near you, that would be enough choosing signals to make the approach.

High Initial Physical Attraction for you is not enough for you to get her phone number, get her on a date with you, and end up in bed with her. It's what you do next, that determines whether you are dealing with an attention whore or a woman that is genuinely attracted to you.

Approaching Without Choosing Signals

The thing with approaching women without her sending any choosing signals is that this could be considered as more masculine since it involves a lot more risk but at the same time it could lead you into unnecessary legal trouble. Women can now have men locked up by merely accusing them of sexual harassment. The chances of you getting rejected are sky high and unnecessary; you will be wasting a lot of time, energy, and money. It could be considered creepy, needy, and you will come across like an eager guy who hasn't got any women showing him choosing signals.

Now here is the caveat, choosing signals or nonverbal approval is just that, approval and she knows it. So keep that in mind. It's good to know how to do both and actually have the balls to approach women without waiting on any choosing signals or nonverbal approval.

The Approach

I'm going to get straight to the point and tell you the unavoidable truth–your "dream girl" won't just show up on your front door and magically start to like you. This might sound obvious, but a lot of men tend to center their lives around this belief. They never go out of their way or make the first move with the woman they like. They work hard to become attractive or desirable, and in their minds, this is enough to entice their dream girl. Life doesn't work like that. Rarely, if ever, do men get approached by women.

As a man, you have to make an effort and approach a woman you like. Life won't just always hand you what you desire. It rarely does. There will always be moments where you have to work for it. In fact, most of the time, as a man, you'll have to work for it.

There are two ways to approach a woman. One is to go direct, using honesty, boldness, and state your intentions and interests right away. The other is to go indirect, under the radar, and slowly lead to your intentions. The first one, the direct approach, is how masculine men approach women, and the second, the indirect and roundabout way of approach, is how feminine women approach men.

The direct approach involves a lot more risk. The direct approach is a huge time saver. You will know relatively quickly if a woman is romantically interested in you or not, and that's exactly what you want. This type of approach feels much more natural for a masculine man. Also, it doesn't feel and look like you are trying to "pick up" a woman, or "trick" here, as you are simply authentic, honest, and bold with her from the start. You are congruent with yourself and your feelings. No tricks, no gimmicks, and no scripts to memorize. Just a pair of big balls. And women love big balls.

The indirect approach is much easier since it involves almost zero risks. Talking to a woman, while hiding your true intentions is manipulative and a covert way of communicating. It's how feminine women communicate and try to avoid rejection—that's why I will only discuss the direct and most effective approach.

When you spot the choosing signals, it's time for action. Be sure that you're in the proper emotional state before approaching her. You need to feel in total control, masculine, sexual, confident, and, most importantly, you need to feel relaxed. If you're acting nervous, scared, and unsure like a little boy, the chances of her giving you her number will drop drastically, let alone getting in bed with her.

If you don't approach her when she is giving you choosing signals, then she will start to doubt your experiences with women. You see, her Initial Physical Attraction for you must be already at least 5,1;

otherwise, she wouldn't look at you the way she did, i.e., she wouldn't give you any choosing signals.

So, when she does, she expects you to approach her, there and then, and show her your balls. I don't mean literally dropping your pants and showing your testicles, but risking her rejecting you. In a way, **risking rejection is what the approach is all about.**

So, you not approaching her when she is giving you the choosing signals will make her think you're either not interested in her (she isn't scoring high on your Initial Physical Attraction), or you're afraid of her because you lack experiences with women. The latter will cause her to immediately lose interest and lower her Genuine Attraction for you. Most women assume the latter is the reason for you not approaching her since most women assume, and like to believe, all men find them physically attractive.

So when you see choosing signals, act on them as fast as possible. As soon as you've made eye contact with her, you need to acknowledge her existence with a relaxed, pleasant, and cocky smirk. Smile with your eyes. Smiling with your eyes is really hard to fake, and it helps to channel your thoughts so you'll seem more sincere.

So what do you say during the approach? Simply make small talk, and after a while, ask for her number. That's it. Simple as that. She will either agree and give you her number without hesitation, or she'll come up with all kinds of lame excuses why she can't give you her number.

Since you approached her because she gave you choosing signals, she will most likely give her number to you.

If you make the approach but don't ask for her number, her Genuine Attraction for you will start to decline. You coming up to her tells her you are interested in her and found her attractive, she knows what's going on, women aren't dumb. So you not going for the number shows weakness. You must always ask for her number! Make sure to save her name in your phone. Don't tell her you will call/text her later—this doesn't meet her need for uncertainty. Just put the number in your phone and make her wonder.

After you have done and master this type of simple and basic approach, you can experiment and have a little more fun with it by taking more risks. **Risking rejection is what the approach is all about.** You can be more direct, bold, honest, and, most importantly, authentic. When you spot choosing signals, approach her, look her directly in the eyes and say the following, or something similar, with a smirk on your face, "You have a fucking unbelievable physique! What's your name?"

Whatever you say, it must be authentic, from your heart, and 100% free from any outcome. Don't say anything about her nails, hair, or shirt she is wearing, since you don't really care about these things; it's not authentic. Be honest and bold; women love men with big balls.

Wait for her response. Do not say your name if she is not asking you for it. If she is giving you a cold answer back, this is a sign of low interest. If she smiles, blushes, and asks for your name, you have to continue the conversation and end it with you asking for her number.

This approach takes a lot of balls since the risk of getting rejected is relatively high and, therefore, can only be done by a true alpha male. Most women will be surprised since the chances are they have never been approached this way. You can be the exception.

Tip: if you are absolutely terrified of approaching women, make it your goal to get rejected. This eliminates any fear you might have and can put in you the not-giving-a-fuck-mood. Go for the rejection; make it your objective. You will be surprised how often you will accomplish the opposite.

But keep this thing in mind; when you decide to approach a woman, you will have a quick, neutral conversation. At the end of the conversation, you will either get her phone number to set up a date or have the interaction end with you getting rejected. This means you will always ask for her phone number, regardless of how low or high you gauged her Initial Physical Attraction for you.

You will never walk away without a) her phone number or b) without you getting rejected. Never leave wondering. Life is too short to wonder what could have been.

You should never "ask" for her phone number; instead, just tell her you want her phone number. "Asking" sets you up for rejection, since it's approval seeking. "Can I have your number?" sound weak. Telling her, you want her number is a more dominant way of getting her phone number. Say something like, *"Hey, I got go, give me your phone number."* Don't say you will call or text her later; make her wonder.

The Phone Game

After the approach, it's time for the phone "game." A lot of books are written on this subject, but I keep it very simple; you can throw away those dumb text-her guides. I, and from now on you, use the phone for one purpose—setting up dates. Not chit-chatting how your or her day was, what she is going to do tomorrow, etc. I don't care how *"times have changed"* and *"everybody is using DM's"*!

If she wonders who is calling or she gets upset why it took you so long, delete her number. These are indicators her Genuine Attraction has dropped to below 5,0 or, worse, it was never there, to begin with.

If you are wondering when to call or initiate contact through the phone, the rule is: wait **five** to **seven** days and ask her out for a weekday. You will **never** ask a new woman to go on a date with you on Fridays or Saturdays. These days are reserved for fun, friends, or women who have proved themselves as being worthy, and women know all high-value men stick to this schedule.

When you are unavailable to meet her on a Friday or Saturday, this will meet her need for uncertainty in a very effective way. In fact, if you are persistent with this rule, and her Genuine Attraction for you is high, she will ask you why you never ask her out on a Friday or Saturday. This is a clear indicator of her Genuine Attraction for you is sky-high, so only after she has explicitly asked you that question will you take her on a Friday or Saturday. But until that happens, always have something to do on a Friday or Saturday night.

After a little positive and fun small talk on the phone, get to the point. Ask her when she is available for a drink. Check your own schedule and set a date. Since you are a busy man, you will always hang up or end the conversation first.

Keep this in mind:

- Set definite dates. Ask if location A at time B would work for her. Pull her into your world. Recommend a place to hang out and set the time you're supposed to meet. Never ask her where she would like to go. Wait for her response.

- If she is unsure or has doubts, take your offer away. Set definite dates!

- Don't text/call in between dates. You are a busy man; you don't use your phone for chit-chatting. Besides, since you have set definite dates, there is no reason to contact her in between dates. Don't double text/call. Wait for her response.

- If she initiates phone conversations with you before the date, just keep it short. Make it clear that you are occupied with your purpose, friends, health, or family at this moment, but you can't wait to see her. I repeat, since you are a busy man, you can't and will not respond immediately to her text or pick up the phone as soon as she calls.

- When you ask a woman a question, you must wait for her response. If she never responds or responds after four weeks, that should obviously tell you how Genuinely Attracted she is to you. There is no need to send her more messages or call her again.

I'd rather not lay out these rules and tell men to play phone "games" with women. But since most men don't have their purpose yet and most men are socially programmed to act in certain beta ways, they will need to "fake it until they make it" and use the rules stated above.

Eventually, when men put their purpose in life first, these things will come naturally.

The Date

During your date, you should focus on these four main things:

1) Being confident and relaxed with the situation.
2) Feeling your sexual energy.
3) Conversing like you've known each other for a long time.
4) Teasing and having fun as much as possible.

My favorite places to meet are at a coffee shop, bowling alley, and miniature-golf course because they have a casual atmosphere, a very public place where women feel safe, and a place where it's never necessary to spend more than a few bucks. So, if you decide to buy her coffee or play miniature-golf, it's never a big deal.

Another benefit of going for a cup of coffee is that it avoids the "formal dating experience" that creates tension. Instead of going somewhere fancy, it's better to go for a venue that's relaxed and comfortable for both of you.

Finally, my favorite advantage of meeting women for coffee, at the bowling alley or the miniature-golf course, is that I can quickly and accurately gauge her Genuine Attraction for me. Attention Whores and women who are Inauthentically Attracted to me hate these kinds of dates, and I mean hate! They expect big, fancy, and expensive dinners. These "cheap and fun dates" are perfect for weeding out women who aren't genuinely interested in you and could save you a lot of time and money. You are welcome.

To pay or not to pay?

That question has been haunting humanity since the beginning of courtship and dating. If you are one of the guys who believe they deserve at least a kiss on the cheek after they have spent money on a woman, read the next sentence very carefully. **Only males who feel inferior to women will feel the urge to compensate for that said gap in value.**

Most beta males see money as something that will set them apart from the rest and is what, they believe, makes them attractive in the eyes of the opposite sex. Money rarely makes a man more attractive; if anything, a weak and eager male with cash is only prone to exploitation by women who are Inauthentically Attracted to them.

Don't try to buy Genuine Attraction; it can't be done, and it is not necessary to spend any money in order to reveal it.

Conversation During the Date

Don't rehearse your conversation. It's not a speech. Try to make it as unforced and relaxed as possible. Try to convey your patience by getting to know more about her at an unrushed pace. Don't over-analyze her words, and don't overthink your own.

Let the women do the talking whenever you're on a date. You can get to know her even when she's the one asking questions by merely observing her reactions to your answers. Talk about her life, observations, interesting facts, current events, or fun stories. Try to agree with her as much as you can without coming off as weak-willed or spineless. What I mean by that is that you should never compromise on your core values. When you compromise on your core values, you miss the opportunity to live powerfully and authentically.

So stay away from topics, subjects, and interests that are often associated with strong beliefs enforced by core values. Stay away from topics like religion, history, race, and politics. When these types of topics arise, just change the subject to something else. Just say something like, "Interesting point of view. Hey, have you heard…"

The reason you want to agree with her is simple; people like others who are like them, who share their views. Most of your friends are very similar to you. Although you didn't agree on some topic at the beginning of your friendship, eventually your friend adopted your views, or you adopted your friend's view. That's what you want with a woman; you want her to adopt your views and submit to your reality. But you can't do that in one session. That takes time, trust, and effort. So it's best that try to agree with her as much as you can without coming off as weak-willed or spineless. Especially in the beginning, so you can build trust. You want to win the war, not the battle.

Playfully tease her every once in a while. Doing this right can really turn the tide in your favor. It shows her how fun and easy-going you are, and this puts her at ease. If you don't tease her, you won't be able to create sexual tension.

A lot of guys don't know how to tease a woman. You need to be relaxed to execute teasing in the right way. You can tease a girl by giving her a silly nickname, pointing out something embarrassing or nerdy about her, or by mimicking and mocking her. You can treat her like a child, disagree with her on something, or accuse her of hitting on you and being sexually aggressive. Don't go overboard though; there's a fine line between teasing and insulting. I always use the line, "Hey, not bad… for a girl." Of course, I have a devilish smirk on my face when I say this.

Topics to avoid during the first date:
- **negative topics,**
- **insults,**
- **putdowns,**
- **complaining or belittling of yourself or others,**
- **planning for the future, things like the second date,**
- **relationship-talk,**
- **your "feelings" for her,**
- **and never, ever brag about yourself.**

Insulting others will only reveal your insecurities. Never put down other people, especially in front of women. Their motherly instincts will be triggered. And not only will they feel sorry for the one you insulted, but they might also start to resent you as well. Planning for the future, talking about the second date, or any relationship talk means certainty, avoid it. Don't start talking about the second date before you've finished the first one. Don't even mention it at the end of the first date. Make her wonder. Internally, you might want to see her again, but your interest in her is conditional upon her good behavior, even after the first date.

Directly verbalizing your good qualities, how much money you make, how popular you are, what kind of car you drive, what you do for a living would qualify as bragging. That means you're a needy guy who craves approval. Displaying your intelligence in order to impress someone is an indicator of low status. Just keep it cool and let her discover these things on her own.

Don't talk about your Ex-girlfriends and don't talk about her's Ex-boyfriends! As soon as that subject comes on, change it immediately. These kinds of topics usually bring up negative feelings because they are loaded with unpleasant memories. You want her to feel good, relaxed and creating good memories with you.

During your first date, don't make another date or talk about the future. This meets her need for certainty, and you want to meet her need for uncertainty and unsureness, remember? This is also the reason why you shouldn't talk too much about yourself on the first date. Let her do the talking!

Affirm the idea that you want to get to know her. Women absolutely love to talk about themselves and passing their thoughts onto others; they just want an interested audience. Be genuinely interested in her. Why would you even go out on a date with a woman if you aren't interested in her in the first place?

Be present with her. Live in the moment. Make her feel special by focusing all of your attention on her, but remember; nothing **negative, insulting, no putdowns, no complaining or belittling of yourself**

and others, and don't plan for the future. This is essential because the moment she goes home, you want her to miss your presence and attention. This will make her wonder and think about you, and this will indirectly meet her need for uncertainty and raise her Genuine Attraction for you.

Finally, the most important thing during the first date; do not talk about your Genuine Attraction for her! Too many compliments are meeting her need for certainty; it let her know where she stands with you. That doesn't create attraction! It creates certainty and is a turn-off.

Give her praise at the start and the end of the date. "Looking good!" at the beginning and "Thanks for the fun times!" at the end.

Remember, a date is not a serious meeting. It's supposed to be fun and exciting. So be playful, relax, and try to enjoy yourself as much as possible.

Touching

A woman typically lets a man know If they're comfortable with physical contact. No one else can dictate the comfort she feels but herself. Her touching you is one basis for her Genuine Attraction for you. The more she's interested and attracted, the touchier she is.

The trick is to let her come to you. Let her initiate all the touching. Only touch her to be courteous (leading her when crossing the street, helping her out the car, etc.) Only when a woman is touching you during the date, begin to reciprocate gradually.

If a woman isn't initiating any touching during the date, it means that her Genuine Attraction for you has dropped, and it might be over for you. Keep this in mind; women need to touch you first during the date. This initial action conveys a high Genuine Attraction. No touching equates to low Genuine Attraction, regardless of how chatty and fun she is during the date. You have to base the authenticity of her attraction to you on her behavior and not her words.

The Kiss

Should you kiss on your first date? Abso-fucking-lutely, yes. If the date is going well and both of you are having fun, and she is relaxed, gazes into your eyes, initiates conversations, laughs, and she is touching you, you must go for the kiss—no ifs or buts.

If her attraction and interest for you are high, she won't reject your kiss. You must go for the kiss during or at the end of the date. It's masculine to go for the kiss and, just like with the approach, risk rejection.

She must understand, and you need to make it clear, without saying it, that the date with her is not a platonic meeting. It's up to you to determine as soon as possible if she is romantically interested in you, or if she's just wasting your energy, time, and money by being either structured or an attention whore by having hidden motives.

If she turns her face so you can kiss her cheek, it means she has little or no romantic feelings for you. Simple as that. If she were into you, she would kiss you. No matter what her excuse is, her actions tell you everything you need to know.

You must go for the kiss even if the date isn't going well and you feel her attraction for you isn't where you think it should be. I have read somewhere that if you go for the kiss on the first date, even if the date isn't going well, it reveals your intentions and your attraction for her too much. It supposedly shows that you aren't capable of reading her body language, her interest level, and have little skills when it comes to dating.

The truth is, if she isn't into you, she will reject your kiss, and if she is into you, she will kiss you back. That's the truth. As a masculine man, you go for what you want in life, even if the possibility exists that it won't work out for you, and you get rejected. You must risk rejection. Just go for it.

Red Flags

Red flags are based on your personal core values and usually arise when a woman has values and morals that contrast your own. They reveal someone's character and could be used to help predict someone's future behaviors and decision-making.

If her behavior and belief system don't match your values, that's already a red flag right there. For example, a tattoo is considered a major red flag by most men on the internet. Why? Conditioning and conformity. Weak people are desperately trying to fit in and belong, even if this would comprise and go against their own personal values.

That is why, for a guy who loves tattoos, these forms of self-expression could be considered as a turn-on or something they appreciate and look for in a partner. It aligns with their personal core values. But for others, a tattoo would be a deal-breaker.

All I'm saying is, don't allow other people's bad experiences to define what red flags mean to you. Define your own. This usually happens along the way and during the process of getting to know each other. That's why it is essential to know and understand what your own core values are.

Here is an example of some behaviors I consider as red flags. If women display any of these behaviors, I consider them a red flag. The more red flags a woman shows, the more I proceed with caution. Nobody is perfect, so don't expect perfection. Nobody can meet ALL your expectations 100%, but you should never ignore the obvious.

1. Does she ask you any personal questions? Is she genuinely interested in you, your life, your history, ambitions, and plans for the future? A woman with low genuine attraction for you will rarely engage in a conversation to get to know you better. In contrast, women who are interested in you will participate and ask personal questions about your life. The difference between the two is that one is genuinely attracted to you while the other is just using you to be seen and attract other men, i.e., inauthentically attracted to you. This would be considered a red flag during the dating process. Another red flag would be questions that would reveal how much money you make/have. For example, questions about your car, whether you are renting or owning a house, etc. These women are clearly not genuinely attracted to you; they are just looking for an ATM. She isn't interested in your character.

2. Does she have a strong conviction? When she read the news, does she have a general sense of right and wrong, even it's not always the popular viewpoint, or do her viewpoints falter too quickly?

3. Does she have a moral compass that's easily influenced by societal pressure?

4. Does she believe that lying is forgivable as long as there's good intention behind them?

5. Does she do what's right, even with no recompense or praise to be had?

6. Does she ever twist facts to gain the upper hand?

7. Does she use emotional manipulation to her advantage? Intentional or otherwise, it's still a red flag in my book.

8. Does she stay true to her word, or does she easily forget the promises she makes? Here are a few scenarios that might sound familiar:

> I.   Promising to do something and falling short on said promise.

> II.   Asking someone to meet and eat or have a drink together with no actual intention of doing so.

9. Does she have a vengeful attitude whenever she receives unjust treatment?

10. Does she have hypocritical tendencies, like judging people who gossip when she herself does so as well?

11. Does she apologize when she makes a mistake or hurt someone's feelings? Does she feel guilty when doing something wrong?

12. Can she effectively communicate her feelings? Effective communication is hard, but essential, especially if you want to spend the rest of your life with them and have children together.

It goes without saying, red flags are only relevant when you consider being with someone for extended or frequent periods of time. If you are just having sex with no strings attached, you can tolerate or ignore most, if not all, the red flags.

The five key fundamentals of this chapter:

- When you spot the choosing signals, it's time for action; approach!
- Use the phone for logistical purposes only.
- Never ask her out on a Friday or Saturday night unless she explicitly asks you.

- During your date, keep it fun; nothing negative, insulting, no putdowns, no complaining or belittling of yourself and others.
- She must touch you during the first date.
- Go for the kiss.
- A date is not a serious meeting! It's supposed to be fun and exciting. So be playful, relax, and try to enjoy yourself as much as possible.

"Fear does not stop death. It stops life."

— Vi Keeland

Part 5: Becoming an Alpha Male: Inner Game

The theory of the alpha-beta hierarchy is a pretty basic and straightforward system. This theory comes from an examination of the group dynamics of certain social animals in the wild and how they manage their social systems. The idea is that one dominant, physically strong, creative, ingenious, and cunning male is at the head of a big pack of males and females, and he has, by far, the most influence on the evolution of that species.

Just like most things in life and because of highly complex human social systems, the blue-pill world considers being alpha context-specific. I believe that by having an alpha mindset, taking the red pill, and living in a free country, men can always remain alpha, no matter what the situation. Because an alpha mindset is internal, no external factors should sway or have any effect on that mindset.

The worldview of a red-pilled alpha male differs on many levels from that of a beta male. First and foremost, red-pilled men are free from the influence of the blue-pilled society. You're part of that society if you lack focus on the truly essential things. This happens if you let your animalistic tendencies hold sway over your judgment and decisions, leaving you stagnant because you're letting your deep-seated insecurities limit your capability.

The role of beta males as a part of the blue-pilled society is to serve. He is first expected to attend school and earn a diploma, only to work in a dead-end job. Then they proceed to squander their earnings for useless things just to impress the people they believe are above their rank. They chase, date, and settle for women sparingly but eventually marry one of them, have children, and get fat and into debt. Finally, the woman comes across an alpha, with whom she cheats on her beta husband and proceeds to divorce him for a better mate. The man, who's just lost half his money and custody of his children, eventually marries another woman using the same strategies that are strongly influenced by the conditioning of our blue-pilled, feminized world. And they are left to the fate of this vicious cycle. Not the red-pilled alpha, though. They walk a somewhat different path.

Control

As we have discussed in the second chapter, everything in the blue-pilled society boils down to one simple thing – control. The blue-pilled world loves to control males. Since their birth, these men have been successfully programmed to do what is expected of them. Red-pilled alpha males are immune to the social programming of the blue-pilled world. A red-pilled alpha male is in total and utter control of his life. He rises above the expectations of the blue-pilled society, giving him the power to do whatever he desires and the freedom and happiness deserving of his rank.

Every day, he does whatever pleases him, knowing that he doesn't need to get the permission of anyone. He gives precedence to his own agenda and ignores the rest, regardless of where they came from.

The red-pilled alpha male is truly free because he is in control of his life, which includes his time, emotions, finances, love life, health (to a degree), security, social life, etc. How does he achieve this? He has an internal locus of control.

Internal Locus of Control

Since the earliest years of our childhood, we have been taught to— and praised for— to assign a cause to our actions and behaviors. It's almost like a reflex. Social psychologists call this attribution theory. This theory is concerned with how people give meaning and explain the causes of behavior, both their own and those of others. An

essential concept in the research of attribution theory is the locus of control, whether one interprets events to be due to one's own behavior or by outside circumstances, factors, and occurrences.

The typical person has an external locus of control. They let outside forces take charge of their life, wholeheartedly believing that their lives depend purely on chance, destiny, fate, or luck. This acts as their scapegoat, enabling their behavior, taking the blame, and responsibility away from themselves whenever life gets hard, or things don't go as planned.

Because people with an external locus believe that success is beyond their control, they let their surroundings and circumstances influence them too much, instead of rising above them. Somebody is always to blame; cultural background, parents, supervisor, friends, government, president, God, climate, past experiences, news, etc., the list goes on and on. This makes them, unknowingly, feel very weak, powerless, and not in control.

These people think pessimistically and lack motivation, not wanting to put extra effort into anything if they're not 100% sure that they'll succeed. They also don't try anything, because they tend to wait for other people to help them out and rescue them.

These people tend to stay on the safe side and shy away from risk-taking to avoid making mistakes. And if they do make mistakes, they place the blame on others instead of learning from them. They believe that all outcomes are mainly dependent on other people, conditions, fate, or luck. These people tend to avoid and prolong taking any decisions. Their beliefs are based on a false premise that if no decision is made, nothing can go wrong!

People with an external locus of control are acting like a victim. Victims have things that happen to them. They view their lives as the cause of their actions. Things happen, and they react.

Many studies have proven that people with internal locus tend to lead more successful lives. This is because they believe the outcomes are the results of their own actions. They believe that they can make anything happen. They have the mindset that putting in more effort begets success. For them, the sky's the limit, and anything they set their mind to, is achievable.

They have the capability of motivating and assuring themselves. Their level of optimism stems from their belief that their fate is up to them, and only them. They take full responsibility for their successes, achievements, and accomplishments in life. But they also take full responsibility for their failures and problems. They tend to explore possible solutions and expect life's ups and downs, wins, and losses. In other words, they believe they are in total control of their lives. Everything in their life is the result of the decisions they've made.

They don't just sit back and wait to be rescued; they do their best to give themselves the best chance of survival.

People with an internal locus of control are victors. Victors make things happen. They view their lives as the effect of their actions. They act, and things happen. Every true alpha male has an internal locus of control.

As human beings, we have a natural tendency to assign meaning to every experience and interaction we have. People with an internal locus of control, assign a totally different meaning to events than people with an external locus of control.

So what does this all mean for you? It means that you need to take full responsibility for everything in your life. And I mean, every-fucking-thing. You need to attribute things internally if you want to improve yourself or change your life for good. You need to make your own decisions, take action, and full responsibility, no matter what happens.

For example:

- Getting bad grades isn't the teachers' fault; you should have studied harder.
- Getting good grades is the result of you studying hard and being a sharp guy.
- You didn't complete a project successfully because the project was easy, or your boss was helpful. It's because you were qualified for the job, and you have worked hard on it.
- When your business fails, don't blame the economic climate. You should have made better decisions and been better prepared.
- When your business idea catches on, it's because you did proper research, came well prepared, and made the right, well-thought-out decisions at the right time.
- When you are late, don't blame the traffic. You should have left earlier, planned better, and/or found a faster route.
- When the second date doesn't go that well, don't blame the woman. You should have used better body language, pulled her into your frame by being more dominant, and not acted goofy.
- When the second date does go well, it's because you did everything right, and you are the man.
- If you feel that you don't earn enough money at your current job, don't wait on your ignorant boss to notice your hard work

and dedication. Instead, go to your boss and ask for that promotion.

- When you lose a game, it's not because the referee wasn't fair. Your team just didn't play that well on that day.

True alpha males are in total and utter control of their lives but, and this is important, not the lives of others. That means they don't try to control or change others by lecturing, setting up rules for other people when in romantic and platonic relationships, being commanding, or trying to change or influence events outside of their control. Red-pilled alpha males only control the controllable, which is themselves, their expressions of their emotions, their time, their money, their health (to a certain degree), etc. (The concept of not controlling the lives of others will be explained in the subchapter. "Rules", page 74)

It is important to note that you should never blame yourself. Nobody is right all the time. When you take control of your life by having an internal locus, you will eventually make some mistakes and make some bad decisions, that's a guarantee. Bad things will happen. It's ok if your previous actions or decisions might not have been right, smart, or wise, but it is essential to understand that you have always done the best you possibly could, given the person you were at that particular point in time.

When you make a mistake, don't dwell on it, just take it as a lesson and learn from it. Because the internal locus of control forces you to look inside and make changes from within in order to achieve the desired results, your fate is in your hands.

"God, grant me the serenity to accept the things
I cannot change, the courage to change the things I can
and wisdom to know the difference."
— Reinhold Niebuhr

"It is possible to commit no mistakes and still lose.
That is not a weakness, that is life."
— Jean-Luc Picard

There are three steps necessary to start developing an internal locus of control and start taking responsibility for your life.

Stop Blaming Others

First and foremost, you have to stop blaming others. You need to stop blaming other people or circumstances, so you can reclaim your power. In other words, start taking responsibility. (But remember; don't be too harsh on yourself.) Blaming keeps you stuck in victim mode. From now on, you won't be playing the victim game.

Stop Making Excuses

The second step is to stop complaining or making excuses. Complaining leads to negative thoughts and eventually back to an external locus of control. Catch yourself whenever you start complaining and make a conscious effort to stop yourself—no more excuses. If there is something that needs to be done, get it done. Don't wait for someone else to do it or some magic to happen!

Start Giving Positive and Empowering Meaning to Events

The third and final step is to give an empowering meaning to everything that happens, and take massive action. Successful people who started from the bottom are self-reliant. They took it upon themselves to better their situation. They took full responsibility for their lives, even when a prosperous future wasn't guaranteed. By creating a ladder of positive and empowering meanings, they've effectively changed the direction of their life.

Now it's up to you to take back control over your life, give an empowering and positive meaning to events, make the right decisions, and take the required actions to achieve the desired results.

Ask yourself the following questions:

- Are you a victim of your life, or are you a victor?
- Do things happen to you, or do you make things happen?
- Is your life the cause or the effect of your actions?

If you have answered yes to any of the above, then you probably have an external locus of control.

> *"A bird sitting on a tree is never afraid of the branch breaking because its trust is not on the branch but on its own wings."*
> — Charlie Wardle

Rules

I believe the concept talked about earlier in this chapter, controlling ourselves and not others, needs a little bit more of an explanation, so here we go.

So, what exactly is a rule? Well, this is a regulation that comes from external sources. For example, laws are rules. The traffic light law is an external factor that is directly governing your behavior. Blue-pilled people love and need to impose rules on others. They set all kinds of rules for their family members, friends, girlfriends, or wives. For example, they don't "allow" their women to hang out with their male friends, flirt with other men, or post certain things on their social media.

These are all rules because they are trying to govern women's behavior. And, looking from the women's perspective, they are an outside source.

You don't want to set up rules for others to follow. That's an ineffective strategy that almost guarantees to disappoint you.

You want to set up standards. These are "regulations" that come from yourself, internally. For example, you value integrity; thus, you'll never tolerate a devious woman who continually flirts with other men or agrees to go on a date with you despite having low Genuine Attraction for you.

What's the big difference between standards and rules? As mentioned, rules are regulations that govern you from the outside. And standards are regulations that come from within. When it comes to personal relationships, rules can and often do extreme damage to your own and your partner's happiness. But high standards will help you become the person you want to be. High standards improve one's life and make a person happy because they align with one's core values. Rules are often forced, inauthentic, and are almost guaranteed to make you miserable. Rules are meant to be broken, leaving you disappointed and angry. Rules take your power away, while standards make you more powerful.

To refer back to the example mentioned above, a woman is free to flirt with other men, you cannot nor should put any rules on women, or men for that matter. But, because you have a certain standard when it comes to flirting with other men, you won't and shouldn't tolerate it. This doesn't mean you are allowed to punish her physically or verbally. You simply remove yourself from the situation or the person that isn't able to meet your standards, after you've explicitly told them about, or they are aware of your standards.

If someone isn't able to meet your standards, it means that you two are just not compatible. Her standards, and thus values, are simply not on the same level as yours. If her standards are set in such a way that the act of flirting when in a committed relationship is not a sign of disrespect, and your standards are the opposite, it might be time to disassociate yourself from that particular person. Lowering your personal standards means you are deviating from your personal values, which in the end won't make you happy, content, or fulfilled.

Dominance

Dominant guys get the girls. Period. If you are not dominant, forget everything else. *Dominance, together with control, is the key to becoming a true alpha male.*

Dominance has absolutely nothing to do with hurting or controlling those around you. Instead, dominance is all about leading others to do what is best, because they can trust you, thus gladly follow your lead and submit to you.

Being dominant makes you feel good, strong, decisive, trustworthy, and it enables you to protect yourself. You take charge of your own life, you get your needs met, and you get to say "No" when the situation asks for it, or you feel uncomfortable. Being dominant prevents other people from taking advantage of your energy, time, and money.

To become dominant, most guys make a mistake and only focus on the outward and physical signs of male dominance. To become truly dominant, you simply take hold of your reality, control it as you see fit, and pull others into it. Read that sentence again.

> *"To become dominant, you simply take hold of your reality, control it as you see fit, and pull others into it."*
> — Stevan Terzić

Most people are unaware of the power of their thoughts and so react to life on "auto-pilot" and unconsciously get drawn into the reality of others.

First, let me explain what reality, or our "truth," really is. This may sound a bit eccentric and unorthodox but bear with me. All of reality exists in your mind, and because of that, there is no objective reality.

The world can be viewed however you want to perceive it. You create the reality that you want, whether you are conscious of it or not. We truly become what we think. Our lives are the result of our own thoughts. More accurately, our lives are the result of our beliefs, formed from our thoughts.

One example would be the placebo effect. Measured in thousands of medical experiments and, in some cases, just as effective as any traditional treatment, a placebo is a phenomenon that can trick your mind into believing that a fake treatment has real therapeutic results. The same is true if you believe that you are ill, you can often produce the actual symptoms of a disease. Vomiting, fatigue, dizziness, headaches, insomnia, and even death could be triggered through belief alone. This is called the nocebo effect.

Our minds are extremely powerful, and what we believe has a significant impact on our behaviors, feelings, emotions, actions, and perceptions. And people tend to respond to perception rather than actual reality. Decades of social psychology research back this up.

Dr. Robert Cleck, a psychologist at Dartmouth College, has devised an experiment that illustrates how powerful our beliefs are. In his experiment, using theatrical makeup, an ugly scar was placed on participants' faces. The subjects were sent into a room for a conversation with a stranger and asked to report how people responded to them with this ugly scar. Right before the participants went into the room, the experimenters said, "Wait a minute! We just need to touch up the scar a bit."

Unbeknown to the participants, rather than touch it up, the scar was removed entirely before the face-to-face conversation with the stranger. Nevertheless, they came back and reported how awkward, unpleasant, and uncomfortable their conversations were, how people they had conversations with avoided looking at their scar and had trouble making eye contact. They also reported the conversation was unpleasant and tense.

Their beliefs about their scar led them to give a specific meaning to a particular situation. In this case, it was negative. Although the scar was only visible in their mind, it was able to bend and shape reality according to their beliefs. Their beliefs created their reality. This means that they responded to their perception and viewed it as their "reality."

Our lives are the result of our beliefs. But for most of us, including you and me, these beliefs didn't just pop up into our minds from out of nowhere. Human behavior appears to be environmentally determined. From the moment we are born, our brain has been programmed with all kinds of beliefs. When we are born, we start with a relatively clean slate. Immediately after our birth, we are bombarded with all sorts of beliefs. Beliefs that came from our parents, siblings, friends, teachers, television, music, internet, etc. They have all programmed us to believe in certain "truths," and thus, as we grow older, we tend to act according to these beliefs.

We are, directly and indirectly, told what we can and cannot do, say, or even think. We are told how to behave, what to fear, what to believe, what to expect, how to love, who to hate, etc. Because of that, as we grew older, we made choices and decisions based mostly on other people's ideologies, without genuinely questioning them.

And most of the other people's ideologies are (unintentionally), harmful and counterproductive. It is only as we grow older; we realize that some of the strategies don't work as promised or advertised. Most of the doctrines hold us back in life. Thoughts stemming from these counterproductive ideologies may sound something like this:

- "I'm not good enough."
- "I can't do it."
- "I can't get that job."
- "She is out of my league."
- "I'm not worthy."
- "People like me, don't do that kind of stuff!"
- "She doesn't date guys like me."

The foundations that each of us supports and base our life on are just simply the beliefs, the conclusions that we've arrived at, based on the rest of the information that we've had presented to us, up until now.

So if we are not continually challenging and re-evaluating or reassessing our own current and personal beliefs in comparison to new information, then we're never going to grow or develop as mature men.

As adults, we need to recognize and get rid of any harmful, negative, and counterproductive ideologies, take control of our inner voice and create our own positive and productive reality. If you don't do this, you will never be able to truly control your reality as you see it fit and pull others into it, which is essential if you want to become more dominant.

Changing your entire belief system is difficult, and most of the time, unnecessary. You'll have to start small, but you must reprogram your mind.

"You act, and feel, not according to what things are really like,
but according to the image, your mind holds of what they are like.
You have certain mental images of yourself, your world, and the people around
you, and you behave as though these images were the truth, the reality,
rather than the things they represent."
— Maxwell Maltz, Psycho-Cybernetics

Creating your reality.

Here is how to do it; first, start **identifying** the thoughts that you have, separate the good ones from the bad ones. Question all implemented ideologies that are counterproductive, negative, and hold you back in your life. Second, **actively motivate yourself** with positive self-talk. And finally, **create your own stable and positive reality.**

Your mind is always thinking, and a lot of our feelings arise from these thoughts. Granted, we cannot always control our thoughts, but we can control what we focus on. Because we can control what thoughts we focus on, it goes without saying that we can control our feelings as well. And it is these feelings and emotions that make us act. Thoughts always come first; emotions always come second. Unless you have some chemical imbalance, all of your emotions stem from your thoughts. This means that you don't have to feel negative, down, or unhappy. **You can always choose how you feel by choosing the thoughts you focus on.** What you focus on, you feel, remember that.

Take control of your self-talk
and create a positive belief about yourself.

If you've received bad news, it's a knee-jerk reaction to be pessimistic, so it requires a bit of work to remain upbeat despite unfortunate circumstances.

If you let external factors control your thoughts and feelings, you have, like most people in the blue-pilled world, an external locus of control. You must try and put a positive spin on every negative situation.

Whenever you are expanding your comfort zone, try to listen to your self-talk, and focus on the feelings you are having. Are they negative, disempowering, and counterproductive? If they are, make a conscious decision that these thoughts will no longer serve you. You have the power to stop those negative and disempowering thoughts that produce those negative feelings, bring you down, and make you stressed. After you've recognized your limiting beliefs, simply replace them with positive and uplifting ideas, beliefs, and thoughts.

Give every negative situation a positive spin and challenge yourself to view things from a positive point of view. For me, the quickest and easiest way to do this is to make the decision to focus on what I can be grateful for. Gratitude is the solution to anger, fear, and doubt.

Another crucial way to view things positively is to simply eliminate all your negative thoughts by identifying the sources of negativity in your life and rooting them out.

Even seemingly trivial things like music or TV shows like news outlets can really put a damper on your mood. The media is the king of programming. Regularly exposing yourself to negativity will eventually influence the way you view the world.

Remove yourself from negative people. Even your close friends or family, if they are negative, they have no place in your life. Negative people will do their best to pull you into their negative reality. You can't allow this to happen.

"Ships don't sink because of the water around them;
ships sink because of the water that gets in them.
Don't let what's happening around you,
get inside you, and weigh you down."
— Unknown

To stay optimistic, you must stop living in the past.

Recalling the bad things in your past will obviously draw out a lot of negative emotions. If you've screwed up before, let it go, because everyone screws up. It's just part of life. Everyone and I mean every single person on this planet earth has something in their past that they are not proud of. The past is all in your head. It's not something that should actively affect your future unless you let it. Contemplate your mistakes, learn from them, and move on. Your past does not have to define you or your future unless you insist on staying there.

"It's okay to look back at the past, just don't stare."
— Benjamin Dover

Talk to yourself by reinforcing positive things about yourself.

Studies show that self-affirmation and using positive language can boost your overall health, help combat stress, and bring more positive energy into your life. It would be stupid not to use this simple yet powerful method that can drastically improve the quality of your life and your reality.

Think of your self-affirmations as a guide that directs you to greener pastures. They give you the right mindset to turn your thoughts into tangible results.

For instance, one of my own affirmations that I habitually do when taking a stroll outside is "I am an alpha male, and I feel comfortable in my own skin. Whatever I set my mind to, I can achieve. I control the controllable. Whatever happens, I can handle it." I feel my shoulders relax, and I start breathing through my abdomen and pace myself better. I instantly feel happier, calmer, and more focused and energetic.

When I say my affirmations, I visualize who I strive to be as a person. It might sound and look silly, but self-talk definitely works. I was skeptical in the beginning, but I had nothing to lose, so I gave it a shot and started reinforcing good and positive things about my life, and I noticed that I began to think differently. I became more positive about life and my future. I can't recommend reinforcing good beliefs about yourself enough. You must try it if you haven't already.

When coming up with your own affirmations, always start with the words "I will" or, better yet, "I am," make them specific, include one or more powerful emotion or feeling words, and, it goes without saying, state them in the positive. You will never speak to anyone more than you speak to yourself in your head. Be kind to yourself.

- *"I am assertive and powerful. I can handle everything life throws at me."*
- *"I am happy and proud that I am taking the time to learn how to become a better man."*
- *"I will handle everything life throws at me. I am capable, smart, and so far, I have survived 100% of my worst days! Nothing can stop me!"*
- *"Whatever happens, I'll handle it!"*
- *"I can tolerate uncertainty because I am in control of what things mean to me!"*

When you first start reprogramming yourself, phrase the affirmations in the present progressive verb tense. *"I don't have full control of my mindset yet, but I'll get there! I know what steps to take and how to achieve my goals."*

When coming up with positive affirmations, try to be realistic. Don't set yourself up for failure by affirming things like, *"I'm a millionaire."* Or *"I'll sleep with 100 women during the next ten days!"*

Remember, affirmations have to be true for your mind to accept them and for you to start believing in them.

"Have you realized that most of your unhappiness
in life is due to the fact that you are listening to
yourself instead of talking to yourself?"
— Martyn Lloyd-Jones

Living In Your Reality

Don't just observe other people's reality and accept it and then adjust yourself to it. Rather, you must create your own strong reality and have your own beliefs about things.

People who don't have the ability to create their desired reality are drawn into the reality of others. And people with a strong and positive reality don't concern themselves with the perception of other people, and their reality often attracts weaker and negative people instead.

So, for example, if someone is being negative or creating unwanted drama, you become a beta and submissive if you enable and agree with their view. You're letting yourself be drawn into their reality.

If you hold fast in your belief and turn the drama into something light-hearted and fun, if you turn negative emotions into positive emotions, then they will be drawn into your reality. This is what I call, at least in my book, true dominance.

As I mentioned earlier, successful people have an internal locus of control. They believe that they can achieve anything if they set their mind to it. Successful people absolutely and without any doubt, believe that they have the ability to succeed. That is their reality, their absolute truth. Their hold on their own reality is so strong that they will not entertain, think about, or talk about the possibilities that they'll fail. They do not even consider the possibility of failure. That's how strong their reality is.

So, in the beginning, you must act as if and honestly believe that you are a high-value man, repeat positive thoughts that reinforce that belief, and eventually, your thoughts will become your reality.

Your mind will increasingly search and find more and more evidence for that belief to be true. As time goes on, your reality will become stronger until there is nothing that can make you doubt your own "truth." When you achieve this, you will always be the most dominant man in the room, a man who is unaffected by any negative external sources and counterproductive, blue-pilled conditioning.

When you start to develop a positive mindset, you will begin to view the world around you differently. Let me give you an example. When a person, with a negative attitude, unconsciously influenced by the ideologies of others, fails at something or, to keep it relevant, gets rejected by a woman, they will view these failures and rejections as reinforcements of their counterproductive, disempowering, and harmful beliefs and behaviors.

When a person, with a positive attitude, fails at something or gets rejected by a woman, they will view these failures and rejections as optimization data. Something they can tweak, adjust and improve, so the next time, they drastically improve their chances of success. This is how you must view the world going forward.

Test, optimize, and, eventually, you will succeed. There no doubt in my mind about that. From now on, in your life, there is no such thing as failure, only feedback, outcome, and a result.

Pull Others Into Your Reality

People will test your reality. This power struggle will be present every single day, from the moment you wake up to the moment you go to bed. You must be aware of this power struggle and be ready to defend your reality at all times.

People who do not have a steady grip on their reality and a clear picture of who they are, what they want, and how they are going to get it, are insecure and not able to be dominant and provide clear direction and guidance to others. Because of this, people doubt them and their decisions, which in turn makes people want to follow someone else, or take over the power and take advantage of them. A leader can't lead if they don't know where they are going themselves.

You cannot allow people to doubt your reality. This also means that you will have to set healthy boundaries and be prepared to protect them at all costs. You will need to discipline people to respect your boundaries and confront those who disrespect or challenge them. More on boundaries later.

The same principles apply when it comes to women in your life. To be dominant with women, you must pull them into your positive reality. It's that simple. You do this by applying two things when interacting with women.

The first thing is, don't let her make any decisions for you. Ever. Period. This means that any radical changes to your plans are intolerable. You need to do this from the start of your interaction with women. Women love it when a man totally owns his feelings, thoughts, who he is, and the fact that they can't change that. This unwavering control of your reality can and will satisfy several of her primal needs.

Another way to pull her and everyone else, into your reality, is to never let her or anyone else, disrespect your boundaries. You need to determine what you will accept and will not accept from other people. Again, to do this, you need to totally own who you are.

When a woman disrespects or mistreats you, you must let her know that she has crossed the line. You must tell her that her behavior is unacceptable. She can either stop exhibiting disrespectful behavior and make it up to you, or you will remove yourself from that situation. If you don't do this from the beginning, she will never respect your boundaries, and you'll never be taken seriously when you try to take a stand later on. You'll live in her reality and always act submissive.

To be dominant always:

- Have a more precise, stable, and steadfast mindset than everyone else.
- Create your own unwavering and robust reality.
- Draw everyone into your reality.
- Refuse to enter the reality of others.
- Set healthy boundaries and protect them.

To be dominant with women, follow the rules stated above and:

- Never let the woman you have (or want to have) a sexual relationship with, make any significant decisions for you.
- Never let the woman you have (or want to have) a sexual relationship with, change your plans.

- Never allow the woman you have (or want to have) a sexual relationship with, disrespect your boundaries without consequences.*

By consequences, I mean you removing yourself from the situation. You don't hit, argue, or yell at a woman.

When in a group setting, always follow these rules to remain the most dominant person in the room:

- You must start to assume dominance over everyone you meet RIGHT away!
- You do this by having a firm hold of your own positive reality and draw everyone you meet into it.
- Without any fear, jump into the leadership position from the start.
- Offer your hand first, and give a firm, strong handshake.
- When talking, maintain solid, unwavering eye contact.
- Take command of the room by speaking consistently and continuously.
- Try to solve group problems.
- Make everyone feel included by seeing yourself as an excellent host.
- Reward people who follow and support you with benefits.
- Be the most relaxed person and remain emotionally unaffected by another's emotions or actions. This demonstrates that your reality is stronger than the reality of others.
- Don't let anything change your perceived reality. If a person is trying to obtain a reaction from you or pull you into their reality, don't allow it.

When in group settings, you need to be a leader, not a boss. What is one significant difference between a boss and a leader? A boss forces people to listen to and obey him by paying, intimidating, or hurting them. People simply must follow a boss, or else.

But people choose to follow a leader. Why? Because leaders have a robust, productive, and positive reality, into which they pull others. They offer benefits for those who follow and support them. They may provide excitement, motivation, wisdom, new experiences, and positive energy, which all create a dopamine rush in someone's mind, keeping them coming back for more.

Leaders have the best wishes of their followers in mind. We all like to surround ourselves with people that make us feel good about ourselves. Most people live a miserable life and are desperately waiting for your shining light to lead the way.

> *"If you want to build a ship, don't drum up the men to gather wood, divide the work, and give orders. Instead, teach them to yearn for the vast and endless sea."*
> — Antoine de Saint-Exupéry

I will reveal to you a trick that helped me tremendously, especially in the beginning, when I first started practicing dominance. Pretend that the whole world is your party. When you host a party, you feel good, confident, fun, and act proactive and assertive. You take the initiative; you are in charge, you are guiding conversations, you bring people together, etc. From the beginning, everybody is drawn into your reality. You get my point.

Act as if you are the host, at all times, wherever you are. The world is yours.

How does being in control and dominant relate to dating?

You have to be in control of your time, at all times! You do that by setting up definitive dates, not leaving any messages, not calling to confirm dates, etc. You don't allow a woman to control your time and pull you into her reality. You must pull her into your reality.

When a woman wants you to confirm dates, her Genuine Attraction is probably not that high. If you go along and agree to call her on the day of the date to confirm it, you are giving up control of your time and are being sucked into her reality, and she knows it. Besides, it creates certainty for her; she knows where she stands with you. Going along with her plans means you are being drawn into her reality; you are acting submissive.

When you set a date, you have to be decisive and in control. Tell her when you are going to pick her up and at what time. What you want to hear are agreeable answers. Anything else means low Genuine Attraction. If you smell any sign of doubt, excuses, or she wants you to confirm dates; she has low Genuine Attraction for you. When a woman has a high Genuine Attraction for you, she makes it easy for you, and she will go along with whatever you suggest, and that's what you want. Her entering your reality, you want her to submit to your fun and positive reality.

So, how should you respond when a woman wants you to confirm dates, or she acts unsure about setting up a date? Take your control back by taking your offer away. She will either agree to meet up at the suggested time, or she'll agree to do it another time. The latter means low Genuine Attraction for you. Delete this girl's number.

You want women who are easy-going, flexible, submissive, and willing to enter your reality. Women who have a high Genuine Attraction for you will gladly get pulled into your reality.

Your Needs & Wants

Because a red-pilled alpha male is dominant and in control of his life, this automatically causes him to make his needs a priority. He is aware that he's the only one responsible for meeting his own needs and making himself happy.

Most of the shy and nice betas out there don't get this. They become paralyzed by their fear, and they're too intimidated by what other people think about them. This hinders them from asking for and going after what they really want. They assume and fear that others will think of them as needy, greedy, selfish, or arrogant. They're afraid of inconveniencing other people by asking for things and then being shown disapproval. On the contrary, people who go after the things they want and ask for the things they desire are viewed as powerful go-getters. And it is only these people who always end up getting their needs met.

Never feel bad for putting your needs first. When you fly on an airplane, the flight attendant instructs you to put your oxygen mask on first before helping others, including children. Adults typically need more oxygen, and in order to be efficient, it's required they put their own oxygen mask on first. It may seem selfish and harsh, but that's how everybody has the best chance of survival. The same applies to you and your life; to be as efficient as possible, take care of your own needs and wants, first. You can't give to others what you don't already have.

In order to effectively get your needs met, you first need to map them out, acknowledge why you have them and how you go about meeting them. To do that, you need to take a look at your personal values.

Personal Values & Standards

Values describe what is important, most valuable in your life. They determine how you go about prioritizing your decisions by pointing out what you stand for and believe in.

Individual standards are based on personal values and influence your actions and behavior.

For example, you value integrity. You believe in being honest and reliable. You think it's important to say what is really on your mind. When you don't speak your mind, you feel weak and disappointed in yourself. Therefore, because you value integrity, one of your personal standards might be never to lie, even if it's to prevent harm or even if the truth could really hurt someone.

One of the keys to living a fulfilling life is to know and honor your personal core values.

Personal values and standards are reflected in the quality of your relationships, your work, and the way you communicate. All people have and live with personal values and standards. But not all personal values and standards have an internal source, meaning some of your values and standards are imposed on you from sources outside of yourself. And because of that, you are not meeting your own needs, the ones you need to fulfill, and that could lead you to feel unfulfilled, and life may seem complicated, awkward, and like a constant struggle.

When people deviate from their core values, they tend to feel bad about themselves. These people tend to often make decisions they later regret because these decisions weren't based on their true core values. Mapping out your values, you will find out what you stand for and believe in, so you'll take more pride in meeting your needs. You won't feel bad or guilty by trying to meet your needs.

Finding Your Core Values

Step 1. Answer the following questions.

- What's important to you in life, and why?
- What sort of story or behaviors tends to inspire you the most, and why?
- What are you most proud of and why?
- What type of stories or behaviors make you angry, and why?

Based on the above answers, some of my personal values are personal growth, integrity stability, sensuality, health and energy, gratitude, meaningful and passionate work, love, connection with others, determination, and peace.

Step 2. Select no more than five values to focus on - if everything is a core value, then nothing is really a priority. You can determine what values you value the most by asking the following questions:

- What value would you easily sacrifice for a large sum of money? Let's say for four million dollars?
- What values are you willing to drop in times of extreme stress? For example, the death of a family member, relocating to a different continent, getting fired or divorced.
- Can you uphold these values in 15 or 30 years? Why?

My new list of personal values consists of health and energy, personal growth, meaningful and passionate work, gratitude, and connection with others.

Step 3. Enforce your core value with personal standards. I will use myself as an example.

Because health and energy are my top core values, I'll now set personal standards to enforce these values. Because I value my health and energy, I make it a priority to get at least seven hours of quality sleep each night, I will never drink any soda, and I will never consume any artificial sweeteners. I must consume at least five portions of fruit and vegetables daily. I must work out at least five days a week.

I won't make an exception, and if I was forced to make an exception, I would be greatly disappointed in myself because the decision to deviate from my personal standards wouldn't be aligned with my top core value.

Write out your core values and some of your personal standards to enforce your values. You don't have to and probably shouldn't do this in one sitting. But do take your time, because these core values will form the basis of your life going forward. Write them down!

Standards

Think about the standards that you currently live by. Are they your own standards? Do you genuinely feel like you're living up to your core values? There's a good chance that many of your current standards have come from outside sources. Meaning, they are not aligned with your core values. Your daily decisions and behaviors might be influenced by someone else's core values. Those external sources could be family members, movies, or anything else in our blue-pilled world. And this must be acknowledged.

Some of these standards may be detrimental to your overall goals and life's purpose. It's time to take a good look at the personal standards that you've set for yourself. And figure out which ones are not serving your best interest. Then you can start making changes by erasing them.

You need to create a set of standards that will guide your life toward the accomplishments that you wish to achieve. Personal standards are incredibly, well, you guessed it, personal. You have to take a good look within yourself and determine what really drives you, what you stand for, what your beliefs and principles are, in all areas of your life. Don't expect to have your standards set in one hourly session or even in one day. Take your time, feel free to adjust, but once you have set your high standards, you need to stay on top of them.

This is a problem for many people. When things begin to get difficult, it's easy to crack and lower your personal standards. Many people are victims of settling. When life becomes difficult, and it will at some point for all of us, it's easier just to give up and feel sorry for yourself instead of working hard to make it over that hump. People find something that's easy, and then just settle for that. These types of people tend to be unsure about their core values.

Setbacks are bound to happen. Problems will arise. But that doesn't mean you should just give up and lower your standards. You shouldn't take the easy way out. You should learn from those setbacks and problems. Figure out a way to turn those negative experiences into positive experiences. Make some adjustments in your life. Be proactive and make things happen.

There are situations where lowering your standards temporarily can be a good idea. For example, let's say your new personal standards are just way beyond reach. When people set unattainable standards for themselves, they tend to get disappointed and discouraged from continuously striving to meet personal standards in other areas of life as well. These types of people go back and forth, lowering and raising their standards their whole life. Because of that, they tend to remain in relatively the same place for years or even fall to new lows in life. Temporarily lowering some of your standards could be a good thing. But when you do, make sure it's only temporary.

That means you should do everything in your power to raise that standard back up, where you really want it to be, so it aligns with your core values. You could do that by gaining more knowledge and accepting that perfection is your worst enemy; it leaves no room for growth. Be willing always to learn and adjust. That way, you are continually growing and improving, while simultaneously, slowly but surely, raising your standards.

Setting your own standards and living according to them means having your own set of values, morals, judgment, belief system, and possessing your own unique character. This is the definition of a man with high value. This way of living will make you unavailable if the benefit you'll gain will be significantly outweighed by what you'd have to put up with. This way of living will make you pickier, meticulous, and will be the leading cause of turning down women, job offers, friendships, etc. if they aren't aligned with your core values. That's the definition of a high-value man.

Boundaries

In order to take good care of yourself and get your needs met, you need to lay down boundaries. And when you do so, do it without apology. You have to take care of yourself; do this without feeling the need to explain or apologize to other people.

See to it that other people consider your needs, wants, desires, and time with due respect. Don't allow others to bring you down or to bully you because of your needs and wants. Insist on what you want—demand what you think is right.

When you start laying down boundaries, people might get offended and probably say hurtful things and bully you. Don't allow it. When you are setting your boundaries, you are basically standing up for yourself. Make people understand that they can't treat you any way they want to. If they try to, there will be consequences—discipline people to respect your boundaries by taking away your attention.

Some people will make it appear that you are in the wrong when you call them out when they violate your boundaries. Instead of apologizing, they will act affronted or insulted. Don't allow their opinions to affect you. Don't allow others to cause you to feel ashamed, embarrassed, confused, or upset. Tell and show people how you want them to treat you.

Tell people what you are willing to do for them – and what you are NOT. Let people know when you feel insulted, hurt, and uncomfortable, or taken advantage of. Never hesitate to say "no." Be firm. Set your terms down without apology. You'll be surprised how most people stop disrespecting you as soon as they encounter a little bit of resistance.

The people you deserve to have in your life will respect you for this. Most people have a sense that they are going overboard when they mistreat you. If you don't say or do anything about it, however, they will view you as weak, take advantage of you, and continue to mistreat you. When you say "no," they will sit up and retreat. They will stop treating you poorly. They will realize that it is time to stop taking advantage of you, hurting you, shaming you, or taking you for granted. They will recognize and respect your boundaries, needs, and wants.

When people intentionally or unintentionally cross your boundaries, you need to stand up for yourself and let them know they crossed the line. Communicate how you feel, citing specific examples, and starting the sentence with "I" instead of "You."

Responding instead of reacting.

Typical beta males go overboard when they realize they need to stand up for themselves and live according to their core values. They usually resort to *reacting* instead of *responding*.

There is a vast difference between the two. A reaction is typically quick, without much thought, based on emotion, tense, and most of the time, an aggressive defense mechanism. A response is thought out, calm, and non-threatening. When you respond, you take into consideration the long-term effects of what you do or say.

The best way of making your point is not with words but by actions. Removing yourself from the situation ensures, most of the time, a life free from drama, hurt feelings, regrets, and lost time and energy.

Here are some examples you could use:

- *"Maybe I wasn't clear. I am not interested in hearing about him/her/that…"*
- *"I would appreciate it if you don't talk to me like that."*
- *"I hear that you really need some help; however, I'm not available to meet your request."*
- *"I understand what you are saying, but I don't agree with you."*
- *"I hear what you are saying, and I understand that you are worried, but I want you to trust that I can make decisions on my own."*
- *"I believe we had an agreement. I clearly made a mistake."*
- *"That's not up for discussion."*

Loving yourself, making your needs a priority, and living by your values is your right. You have to live your truth! Go out there and get your needs met, lay down boundaries, and protect them by learning to say "no."

Words Of Caution

Being dominant, making your needs a priority, living your truth, and setting healthy boundaries come at a cost.

Being dominant, standing up for yourself, and setting healthy boundaries make you feel outstanding about yourself. You feel happier. You feel stronger. You get a jolt of energy and energize the people around you. It gives you the chance to live a more comfortable and more fulfilling life, but there is a downside to being dominant and living your truth, and it's something that I feel needs to be discussed. By the way, this does not mean that you should not become more dominant, make your needs, and wants a priority, and set healthy boundaries. It merely means that you should be aware of the potential consequences you are likely to encounter.

Prepare to be mentally, emotionally, and physically strong.

In times of difficulty, people instinctively turn to a strong person for direction and help. People will expect you to lead and guide them. They will seek counsel and advice from you. They expect you to make decisions for them. They will depend on you for help and assistance. A dominant alpha male is a leader. You have to be strong and tough to assume this role. You have to be able to think fast and act decisively. The position can be tiring and draining. Sometimes, you wish to be on the other side of the fence. You want to look up to someone to decide for you or tell you what you should do. You want to have someone to turn to and to give you support or approval. As a dominant alpha male, you are on your own. The buck stops with you. There is no one to turn to. There will be times when you feel lonely.

Don't feel overwhelmed by the power that being alpha bestows on you. Enjoy the command and control. Recognize the fact that you are a dominant alpha because you have the abilities and skills for the role.

And the people need a strong leader like you. You are astute. You are strong. You can make the right decisions – for yourself, as well as for your "pack." You don't need someone else's go signal or approval.

Prepare to be criticized, scrutinized, and judged.

People will criticize you – and some of the criticism may hurt you badly if you allow it to. The foremost world leaders are alphas. They are recognized for their leadership, not for their popularity. In fact, many of them are very unpopular.

They are always in the limelight – and not always for pleasant things. People scrutinize them, put them down, make fun of them, and fight with them. People criticize them for almost everything they do or say, their leadership styles, their political pronouncements, etc. You will experience some of this unpleasantness when you assume the role of a dominant male leader. People will disagree or differ with you. Some will say mean and cruel things about you. Some will try to tear you down. Some who want your power for their own will undermine your reputation and sabotage your leadership. Dominant women will want you to submit to them as all other beta males do. These women will insult you every chance they get.

Don't expect everyone to sing your praises. You will make a lot of enemies. You will experience a power struggle, just like I talked about earlier. The tallest tree always experiences the strongest winds.

Prepare to chip away at some of your relationships.

When you set boundaries, you stop other people from taking advantage of you, bossing you around, and disrespecting you. This does not mean that everything will turn peach-perfect in your life. This does not mean that all your relationships will become rosy.

You still can't control how other people will think, feel, or act about this turn of events. Not all your family and friends will take kindly to your being more dominant and, most won't agree or accept your positive and upbeat reality. Some will disagree with and even dislike you for it. Some will resent you; they will react adversely to the resultant balance of power. You might also lose some friends in the process. Good, you don't need those kinds of people in your life, anyway.

Fear

Fear comes in many forms. Most common is the fear of rejection, disapproval, embarrassment, fear that we're just not enough, etc.

Beta males let fear control their lives. Fear paralyzes them and not just in their relationships, but in other aspects of their life. This is why beta males will never find the success they desire even if they're capable of achieving it.

The reason most men never confront their fears is that they fail to realize that it's all internal. Since beta males have an external locus and believe they are not in control of their life (read the previous chapter), they believe fear stems from external factors. They wait and hope for their fear to magically disappear instead of taking responsibility for their fears. They comfort themselves by thinking, "I'm sure these feelings of anxiety will eventually pass, and when it does, I'll be swimming in women!"

Let me tell you a little secret; everybody feels afraid when they enter a new, unfamiliar situation. It's a normal part of the psychological reality of human beings. **Fear is a form of protection, warning us of potential danger. It's not supposed to be something that limits us.** An alpha male knows this, giving him the ability to be in total and utter control of his life.

What separates beta males from the alphas is how they deal with their fear. The only way to "get rid" of the fear is to do the things you want—i.e., approach women, ask for a raise, say no, ask for her number — despite the fear. You have to face your fears head-on. If you back off, you will always stay stuck in your current lifestyle - alone, masturbating to porn, and never get the things that you desire. You **must** confront your fears. There is no other way. The truth is your fears will never go away. As long as you challenge yourself, keep doing things in life that excite you, and expand your comfort zone, you will always experience new fears. We all do. It's what we do after we feel fearful that determines if these fears control us or we control them.

"The oldest and strongest emotion of mankind is fear,
and the oldest and strongest kind of fear is fear of the unknown"
– H.P. Lovecraft

Humans grow when they are in a state of discomfort, and when they are expanding their comfort zone. Just think about; the oldest and strongest emotion of mankind is, indeed, fear. If our ancestors of the hunter-gatherer age didn't confront their fears, you probably wouldn't be reading this right now.

I heard from a Ted Talk by Bill Eckstrom, *Why Comfort Will Ruin Your Life*, that discomfort and expansion of our comfort zone can be set in motion from three things; we are either 1) involuntarily exposed to pain and discomfort, 2) someone helps us get through discomfort, or 3) we consciously and voluntarily choose discomfort. Let me give you an example.

Getting fired from a job would be considered a forced and involuntary expansion of your comfort zone. You must now go out and get a new, preferably better job. You might decide to finish school and get that degree you always wanted.

Teachers, parents, or coaches can help us expand our comfort zone by supporting us and offering different points of view. They might even push us just enough to push through the fear.

When we decide that enough is enough, and we consciously make efforts to change and improve our lives for the better, make a statement, or voice our opinion, all this would be considered an expansion of our comfort zone by choice. People who practice stoicism call this exercise voluntary discomfort.

People who never get out of their comfort zone are driven by safety and self-preservation. They stay stuck in life. People who do get out of their comfort zone are driven by progress and growth. Because of that, only these people tend to actually grow, improve, and achieve.

When you first practice the expansion of your comfort zone, your brain will send you signals of pain and discomfort. You will recognize these signals and interpret them as fear. Your mind will start to rationalize these fears and come up with really good excuses on why not to do it. If you always give in and allow this set of rationalizations and excuses to hold you back, you will never expand your comfort zone. For example:

- "I look like shit now; I won't approach her today."
- "I don't know what to say; I will approach her tomorrow."
- "I'm tired now; I will approach her when I am well rested."
- "She is with her friends; I will approach her when she is alone."
- "I can't start my own business; I don't have enough time."
- "I can't go to the gym; it's raining."

So next time you feel discomfort, and your heart starts to race, palms begin to sweat, remember this is your chance to grow. Embrace that moment, because it is the only time you actually grow as a human being. This is how you grew your personality as a child; why stop now?

"Courage is being scared to death, but saddling up anyway."
– John Wayne.

I encourage you to actually consciously choose discomfort and actively expand your comfort zone. Start small and work your way up. Take a different route to work or try new food. Join a gym or learn a new skill. Take cold showers, abstaining from masturbation for long periods of time, or try to fast for a day. Ask for a raise, ask women out, have a threesome, and try those kinky sex positions you always wanted to try. Sometimes you just have to think, "Fuck it!" and go for it. Get comfortable being uncomfortable.

These exercises will act as appreciation boosters and are a great way of training your willpower and handling your fears.

To make your social interactions with women a bit easier and to control your fear of approaching women, you need to have this attitude:

Have no expectations — the worst thing that could happen is that she could say no. Big fucking deal! Alphas view women as sources of fun and sexual pleasure in life, no more, no less. Do not focus on relationships, commitment, sex, or what might or might not happen. Keep it fun, lighthearted, and sexy.

Do it repeatedly — approach as many women as possible. The ones you are attracted to and the ones you find less attractive. Practice. Regularly and frequently, confront your fears head-on.

If you don't approach her, you are guaranteed to fail. Most of our fears and anxieties aren't genuine fears at all. Most people mistakenly interpret the feeling of excitement as fear and anxiety. And therefore, they interpret it as proof of weakness and inadequacy. Excitement can easily convert into strengths, while fears, most of the time, reveal our weaknesses and insecurities.

Next time you catch yourself letting fear control your actions, confront it head-on. Ask yourself if it's fear you are feeling, or are you feeling excited because you're doing something new? If you are not in immediate physical danger, it's probably excitement.

"A ship in harbor is safe, but that is not what ships are built for."
– John A. Shedd

Being Alone

In our modern, blue-pilled world, being alone is seen as a thing to be avoided and shunned. People who prefer the company of themselves are often portrayed as socially awkward, self-obsessed or energetically, and intellectually unrelatable to others.

I will argue the exact opposite of this, spending more time alone, not only increases your social status but also help you get to know yourself better, achieve spiritual awakening or enlightenment, and could help you help achieve your long-term goals more quickly and efficiently by resolving difficult problems.

By being alone, alphas realize that they don't have to be around annoying people, energy-vampires, or be in bad and non-sexual relationships with women.

The ability to be alone gives alphas a power other people don't have. Most people would rather be around people they don't like because they fear disapproval and loneliness. They will stay in unhealthy, platonic relationships because they are afraid of not being able to find someone better — not alphas.

As an introvert, I enjoy being alone. It gives me the freedom to think, reflect on myself, and my life direction. It gives me time to concentrate on my purpose and come up with solutions to all kinds of problems.

It is important to note that being alone doesn't mean you're a loner or a people hater. Positive social interactions make us happy, and belonging to a group is one of our human needs. Balance is key.

If you are an extrovert, you need to learn how to be alone and be perfectly fine with it. Focus on your purpose, health, or occasional entertainment when you are alone. Try to get to know yourself during your alone time.

If you are an introvert, you need to learn how to enjoy being with people and expand your social circle. To do this, all you need to do is take a genuine interest in others and be proactive.

Genuine interest

Try to learn a person's likes and dislikes and match your actions and words with this information. Pump them up with your own optimism. Don't come off as someone negative. No one wants to hang out with a downer.

Let your friends talk about what they want, do things they like, and simply listen. Alpha males aren't needing or continually craving attention. They don't have to brag about their accomplishments or steer the topic towards themselves because they are self-assured.

Make the other person feel important and become genuinely interested in other people.

Being proactive

Lastly, try being proactive. Take the first step and invite others to hang out instead of waiting for them to call you. People with no friends or loners are passive and believe that it is up to other people to come to them and make the first move. I hope you've realized that people with an external locus of control belong to this group of people. We have discussed this in the previous chapter. They wait for others to influence their lives.

Some people are just too shy or lazy to take the initiative, so do it for them instead. Take control of your own social life by being your own personal coordinator. Because you are in control of your life, you must be the one to take responsibility for everything that you do, and that includes activities with your friends.

Master the ability to be alone, and you will never act needy again.

"Be alone, that is the secret of invention; be alone, that is when ideas are born."
— Nikola Tesla

"If you make friends with yourself, you will never be alone."
— Maxwell Maltz

Masculinity

Masculinity is an inherent quality of men that aids their chances of survival, whether as part of a group or on their own. Without masculinity, our species wouldn't have survived up to this point. It empowers men to shape the world as they see fit and to produce offspring that continues their lineage. It also prompts men to provide for the needs of their loved ones and to protect them from potential danger. Masculinity begets desirable qualities like discipline, strength, passion, courage, integrity, and perseverance. But be aware that too much masculinity has adverse effects, giving you a propensity for destruction, brutality, and aggression. Becoming truly masculine means accepting all these traits, be proud of them, and use them wisely.

To get a better understanding of what true masculinity is, we must first understand and know what masculinity is definitely not. Masculinity has nothing to do with your muscles, strength, skill set, physical strength, and athletic capabilities. Although these traits are highly encouraged and promoted as masculine, especially in young boys, they certainly don't make one more of a man. In the blue-pilled world, economic success is also often seen as an indicator of one's masculinity. This is false because we can't measure what a man is based on his job title, position, net worth, or amount of possessions he has accumulated. This way of thinking can become toxic, unproductive, and, if taken to the extreme, self-destructive.

Masculinity's main hallmark is stability, the complete opposite of femininity, which represents change and disparity. Feminine energy desires constant change instead of stability. Masculine essence and energy are primarily driven by direction in life, or, to be more specific, masculine essence and energy are primarily driven by a never-ending life mission and the lessons learned by overcoming the challenges along the way. The feminine essence is moved primarily by emotions, intimacy, and connection. Masculine energy tends to forgive and let go while feminine energy tends to hang on and remember.

What does this mean for you? It means two things.

First, as a masculine man, **you must be committed to a cause**, your purpose, something that is preferably changing the world for the better.

Second, as a masculine man, **you can't be moved off your center**, your purpose, goals, and the cause you are committed to. Especially not by ever-changing and turbulent feminine energy.

Because of the fact that a masculine man can't be moved off his center, he is emotionally consistent, centered, and steady. It's this consistency and the drive towards a specific goal that gives feminine energy, a woman, most of the time, a feeling of safety and certainty. You achieve this by being in control of your life, knowing what you want and how to get it.

Masculine energy is all about getting things done despite any setbacks, obstacles, or barriers. This applies to your life purpose as well as to your small, daily tasks and goals like gym, dates, school, washing your car, hanging out with family or friends, etc.

A masculine man is driven by facts rather than his feelings. A masculine man doesn't hide his emotions; he controls emotional expressions. This means he doesn't cry in public or freak out in public when he gets mistreated in a store. This means he doesn't bombard the girl with five messages, because he doesn't let his emotions take over and make decisions for him. He is well aware of his feelings, he knows why he is feeling a certain way, but most importantly, he always responds and never reacts.

A life ruled by facts is one that is stable, anchored, and constant. A life ruled by feelings is one that is turbulent, unstable, ever-changing, and stormy.

A masculine man doesn't hide his natural manly desires, like being sexual. There is absolutely no valid reason to apologize for and hide your high sex drive the way beta males do. Alpha males feel no shame in their libido; they instead flaunt it with pride.

This type of energy attracts feminine women and feminine energy in general. Feminine women want that feeling of safety from being with a masculine man. A man who can't be moved from his center is a man who is able to protect, lead, and provide. A man who is able to make those difficult decisions and can be a source of emotional strength and stability she, or whoever needs it, can always fall back on.

To become more masculine, spend some time with other masculine men that you look up to. Ideally, young men should spend more time with their fathers. If this is not possible, find another (fictional) masculine role models and emulate their behavior.

Forgive your father and break free from his expectations, or better yet, and, if possible, improve the relationship with your father. Young men, especially ones who were abandoned by their fathers, or the ones that didn't spend much time with their father, tend to lean more to the feminine spectrum. They are more violent, unsure, unforgiving, and tend to be emotionally unstable.

They tend to have more difficulties with social adjustment and tend to have an intimidating persona in an attempt to disguise their underlying fears, bitterness, resentments, anxieties, and unhappiness.

Most men waste their entire lives trying to please their demanding and seemingly never satisfied and proud father. If you are a grown man, it's time for you to break this pattern by embracing your father's efforts and love. Your father is at some level, just doing his job; challenging you to become a better man. Since masculine energy is calm and tends to forgive, it is essential to improve the relationship with your father. If that is not possible, at least try to forgive him.

Your feelings towards your father might be unconsciously forcing you to embrace your feminine energy — time to deal with it. Try to learn as much as you can from your old man, move on, start to carve out your own path, and think your own thoughts.

Challenges And Confidence

Masculine energy grows through successfully overcoming challenges, no matter how small or big. Overcoming challenges and "winning" has been proven to give men a little testosterone boost. Testosterone, often blamed as the catalyst for aggression, lowers stress in men, improves our mood, and makes us calm and more levelheaded. Higher natural testosterone levels make men more emotionally stable and strengthen our ability to make better and more rational decisions.

A lot of self-help books tell us that we should "just be more confident." This is blue-pill world thinking. Confidence is not something you can turn on like a light switch. Confidence is a byproduct of successful achievements, not the cause of it. This means you must act.

To build up your confidence, you must first have small wins. To have small victories, you must first make an emotional decision and firmly decide that you must achieve a certain goal. The second step is to just take action. No ifs or buts. Just fucking start. And lastly, you must risk failure while expecting a positive result. In other words, you must believe in yourself. Thus, to build up confidence, you first must have courage.

Courage means to have the ability to do something that frightens you, to do something despite the fear. In order to do that, you have to learn how to deal with uncertainty in your life. When you learn how to tolerate uncertainty, the world of possibilities will open up to you. A simple way to tolerate uncertainty is to develop an internal locus of control. Something we have discussed at the beginning of Part 5. It all boils down to this: the meaning you assign to any event, interaction or outcome defines the emotional tone of your experience and the feelings you generate throughout your life. While we cannot control the events or circumstances of our life, we can absolutely control our reactions and the meaning we give to our experiences.

When it comes to your confidence, it's difficult to get the ball rolling, but when it starts to move, it's like a snowball. After initial success and small bursts of testosterone and confidence, all you need to do to stay confident at all times is to reinforce positive beliefs about yourself and your small/big achievements, have a little faith, keep taking calculated risks, and stay focused on your purpose and goals. By achieving success, no matter how small or big, and by focusing on your mission at all times, your confidence will always be on the rise.

To become more confident, do the following:

- Decide where to direct your focus, take action, embrace your challenges, and risk failure while expecting a positive result. Believe in yourself by creating your own strong reality. Realize you can tolerate uncertainty because you control the meaning of the events.

- Eventually, you will succeed. Small wins count. Solve problems in your life, start from fixing your car, making your bed, getting that degree, etc. Never procrastinate, just get it fucking done.

- When you succeed, reinforce positive beliefs about yourself and your small/significant achievements. Don't focus on your failures. The meaning you give to your experiences will always change how you feel — and the emotion you feel always becomes the quality of your life.

- Keep making emotionally driven decisions, keep taking actions, have faith in yourself, and risk failure.

In case you forgot, true alpha males have an internal locus of control, which is mine, and now yours, secret in life. Internal locus of control makes all of this possible.

Emotional Stability

Learn to recognize and effectively label your emotions. You must have the ability to know what you are experiencing. Is it nervousness, sadness, anger, grief, or joy? Why do you feel like that? Try to control your emotional expression by acknowledging your emotions in time. This does not mean you should never cry, feel sad, or unhappy. All emotions are natural and should be embraced, processed, digested, and adequately handled. They just need to be expressed at the appropriate time.

The eight key fundamentals of this chapter:

- Be in control by having an internal locus. Control only the controllable.
- Be dominant by pulling others into your frame. Defend your personal boundaries.
- Know and understand your values and standards.
- Put your needs first; take full responsibility for them and live your truth.

- Expect criticism. No matter what you do, you are sure to be criticized. Even if you are trying to bring about a positive change in your life. Especially if you are trying to change for the better in the presence of people who aren't happy, content, and fulfilled.
- Never allow fear to control your life. Confront your fears head-on and use them to your advantage.
- Master not only the ability to be alone, but to actually enjoy being alone.
- Embrace your masculinity and what it means to be a man; committed to cause and become unmovable from your center by being determined and emotionally stable. Be driven by facts rather than your feelings.

Part 6: Nonverbal communication

It is essential to make a distinction between nonverbal communication we can control, nonverbal communication we can't control, and nonverbal communication in between. Let me explain.

Nonverbal communication we can't control is our genetics, height, jawline, the color of our skin, eyes, etc. Nonverbal communication we can control are things like our hairstyle, facial hair, nails, fashion style, fitness level, voice, and body language. Nonverbal communication in-between consists of things like our body odor, skin health, teeth, and body type.

Why is nonverbal communication important? Our nonverbal communication tells others how 1) we feel inside, 2) how healthy we are, and 3) our intentions. Let's tackle all of these, one by one.

Nonverbal communication we can't control

Do genetics matter? Yes, they do. I would lie if I said your genetics didn't matter because they really
do. People who are blessed with good genes and are considered conventionally physically attractive have an advantage when it comes to dating, making friends, and life in general.

Women prefer dominant-looking men, especially near ovulation. Features like a squared or wide face, strong jawline, pronounced eyebrows, a full beard, large Adam's apple, thin eyes and lips, hard body, broad shoulders, and big arms—are considered more dominant and attractive by most women. All of these features represent more testosterone. Which in turn represents, on a primal and subconscious level, a healthy, strong, and capable man who can provide and protect himself, his women, and their offspring.

On the other hand, features such as a round face, big eyes, small eyebrows, full lips, soft body, and an hourglass figure—tend to be considered stereotypical "feminine" features.

Now, you have to realize that it's not only women who regard our appearance as a determinant in establishing our societal rank and individual roles. Men do it just as much as women. Judging others based on their external appearance is, unfortunately, deeply ingrained within our behavior as humans. In a paper written by researchers from the School of Business Administration at the University of California, Riverside, men with wider faces, when in negotiations, statistically come out ahead in terms of money by quite large margins.[3]

In similar research written by the same authors, it was found that men with wider faces tend to run corporations with stronger financial performances. These men could only achieve these results if they were assertive, dominant, capable, and driven, not because they possessed a wider face.

It could be argued that men with wider or more masculine faces, get treated differently by others and because of that have fewer or different kinds of obstacles on their way. But, I'm convinced that without the necessary attitude, skills, and drive, the men in this study wouldn't be able to achieve the results they did.

Certain physical features determined by your genes are all about what they, sometimes falsely, represent to others on a primal and unconscious level; our health, mineral content, hormone levels, capabilities, intellect, etc. Now, we can't do much about our jawline and the width of our face, but we can control how we act and respond. At the end of the day, it is our behavior that determines our outcomes. We might not achieve the same results as quickly as if we were blessed

---

[3] https://www.eurekalert.org/pub_releases/2014-07/uoc--wmn072314.php

with better genetics, but I genuinely believe it is our duty to become all that we can be by reaching our full potential.

So if you are unhappy about certain genetic traits you possess, and it isn't much you can do about them, the only option left is to accept them and turn them into strengths. As an alpha male, you fully accept yourself, have a positive attitude, and control the controllable. You improve the improvable.

The goal in life is not to bullshit and lie to yourself, but to see reality for what it actually is, and then if possible, proceed to make some changes, adopt different kinds of strategies to get an advantage or an edge, and achieve the desired results. Not to complain about things you have no control over.

You have to make the most of what you've got. You have no other options. You just can't do anything about your physical features determined by your genetics. You can't change your height or the length of your jawline. Stop wasting precious time on things you can't control. Suffering is the mind's refusal to accept reality as it is.

At the end of the day, looks only open up the door. They don't keep you in the room. If you aren't capable, driven, focused, or don't have the necessary skills, mindset, and attitude to run the company, meet a women's needs or keep that spark in your relationship, you are, sooner or later, out.

Nonverbal communication we can only influence

Your body odor, skin health, teeth, and your fitness level are things you can improve. Although the improvement will be limited, nevertheless, it will still be beneficial. It goes without saying you should take excellent care of your teeth by cleaning them properly, by brushing and flossing. Regular visits to your dentist are essential. Try to fight or reduce your body odor. The best way to reduce body odor is through prevention. For most of us, proper hygiene - like washing well and applying an underarm antiperspirant or deodorant - should be enough. For some, extra measures, like changing diets, will be necessary. Always see a doctor or a dietician before making any drastic dietary changes.

Your skin is the most prominent part of your body. It is also your body's largest organ that signals a lot about your health. Both internal and external factors affect skin condition and influence how it looks. Some of these factors cannot be influenced, but many can. Careful and smart skincare can protect your skin and keep it glowing and looking healthier and younger for longer. According to psychologists at the University of St Andrews, Scotland, eating more fruit and vegetables will make you more attractive to the opposite sex. They reported that humans find the skin of someone who consumes large quantities of carotenoids healthy-looking and "attractive." Plants produce carotenoids as protection against sunlight.[4]

Nonverbal communication we can control

You need to dedicate some time and energy to improving your health and appearance by mastering nonverbal communication you can control. You can manage your hairstyle, facial hair, nails, fashion style, fitness level, voice, and body language.

I won't go into detail about how you should dress or cut your hair and how much or how little facial hair you should have, that is a personal preference. But don't shy away from getting professional help if necessary. Your style, haircut, grooming, and how you smell, all say something about your self-respect, and therefore, must be in line with the message you want to communicate. There's no right or wrong. It's all about context. You should dress and look appropriate for your age,

---

[4] https://www.sciencedirect.com/science/article/abs/pii/S1090513810001169? via%3Dihub

career, and situation. If you look like a bum, people will treat you like a bum. If you look like you just escaped from a mental hospital, don't expect people to treat you differently. I'm not saying that's right or wrong; I'm just saying how it is. Human beings are predominantly visual creatures, so most of us judge others by their looks.

Your health, attractiveness, and the message you are trying to convey are intrinsically connected to your fitness level. And you have to do everything you can to preserve your innate healthy fitness levels. A wispy, stick-thin guy or a morbidly obese man who can't even walk up a flight of stairs without getting out of breath has zero chances of getting into the unplugged lifestyle. No woman will want to be with you if you don't take, at least, minimum care of yourself.

I'm not qualified to give medical advice, so no information in this book should be considered medical advice. You should consult with a healthcare professional before starting or changing any diet or exercise program. If you have or think you have a medical problem or symptom, please consult a qualified physician.

Do some resistance training to keep your muscles in top shape.

Getting ripped offers a ton of benefits - you gain an edge in masculinity by stabilizing your hormones, become more comfortable and confident in your body, your mental sharpness, and your energy levels are boosted. You don't necessarily have to take it to the extreme unless this is on your checklist. Simple resistance training, like weightlifting, can do wonders for your appearance and stamina. Even a light workout with higher reps will show good results if you do them correctly and consistently. Still, I recommend going hard for 45 minutes six days out of the week, with every day training different muscle groups to complete exhaustion. This will keep every part of your body at its full potential.

Lifting heavy weights is the best form of exercise to boost testosterone. Another effective way of increasing testosterone is through high-intensity interval training (HIIT). Regular endurance exercise also called aerobic activities (such as cycling or running for hours) had been shown to decrease testosterone levels. Always consult your physician before beginning any exercise program.

Sleep eight hours a day.

Sleep doesn't just help your physical fitness; it also keeps your mental and emotional faculties in their normal state. Plenty of people make the mistake of not sleeping the full eight hours, and the effects are detrimental: depression, fatigue, dulled senses, increased insulin, memory loss, anxiety, bad skin, and I could go on and on. Not sleeping enough increases the risk of cardiovascular disease, which can restrict blood flow to the heart, the brain, and the penis, and you don't want that.

Insufficient sleep can affect hormone production, including growth hormones and testosterone. If you're one of these men, make it a priority to change your habits, and you will see how much your life will change for the better.

Keep your natural testosterone levels high.

Testosterone affects men from their physical strength, mood, and cognitive function to their virility. Being a sex hormone, it also influences the way we think. As mentioned earlier, the relationship between hormones and behaviors can be bidirectional. This means that hormones can influence behavior, and behaviors can influence hormones.

You can raise your testosterone levels by merely changing your eating habits. Avoid heavily processed food that's loaded with preservatives and nasty chemicals that may increase your estrogen levels. Their adverse effects might not become immediately apparent, but let me tell you that everything accumulates, and you'll only notice them when it's too late. An example would be sugar substitutes and artificial sweeteners.

I found out that most pre-workout and protein powders contain one or even two kinds of artificial sweeteners. I swore off them and replaced flavored protein powders with naturally sweetened supplements. I replaced pre-workout powders with regular coffee and pure powders without any additives.

Eat mostly unprocessed, natural, fresh foods: meat, seafood, a lot of vegetables, legumes, nuts, berries, tubers, and fermented foods. Stay away from sugars.

Do your research.

Go out and buy some books and then seek professional medical advice. Make sure the information is coming from reputable sources. This is extremely important. As mentioned earlier, it's hard in our monetary system to trust people. Almost 90% of all the information you will find on the internet is marketing and promotion. Both have the same end goal: to increase profits for their business. Don't take medical and fitness advice from unqualified steroid users on social media.

You can never have too much (quality) information when it comes to improving your well-being. The sooner you get into the mindset of taking your health into account, the sooner you can reap the countless benefits I have mentioned. Keep yourself updated when it comes to your health and fitness. There are always new discoveries being made; new research is constantly coming out, revealing new life-changing information and debunking old myths.

Two habits that have made a profound difference in the quality of my life are juicing vegetables and intermittent fasting. I would strongly suggest you learn more about these habits.

Alpha Male Body Language

The majority of human communication is transmitted non-verbally. A University of Pennsylvania study reported that a whopping 70% of human communication is body language, 23% is voice tone and inflection, and only 7% is spoken words. I'm not sure how much of that is actually true, but I do know for a fact, that body language accounts for a lot of communication, especially when it comes to dating and seduction.

Body language is an outward reflection of our state of being and emotions at a particular time. It is also considered the most honest form of communication because the body rarely if ever lies. It would take a significant amount of effort and energy to fake this nonverbal communication.

It is common knowledge that women are far more perceptive than men, and they tend to have an eye for detail. They are far better at deciphering nonverbal communication than men are, mainly because of evolutionary reasons. Women are far more alert, aware, and responsive to body language. Better yet, when it comes to attraction, they can spot both dominant and submissive body language from a mile. That is why you need to learn how to display proper body language that attracts women, and you need to develop basic skills at deciphering the body language of others.

Women are attracted to dominance on a primal level; it can trigger their biological sexual desires. Real dominance must be demonstrated by nonverbal **and** verbal communication, and that's why it is crucial that what you feel, think, and say must match what you display with your body.

By exhibiting proper body language, to be more specific, dominant body language, you will automatically appear more masculine and thus attractive in the eyes of every female you come across. This does not mean they will automatically develop a high initial Genuine Attraction for you, but it will significantly increase your chances.

There are many, many books written on body language. Some of them are silly; others are quite good. After fifteen years of trial and error and a lot of studying and reading, I have a good foundation for what I believe is considered dominant body language that is most effective when it comes to attracting feminine women.

For me, the best and easiest way of exhibiting dominant body language was to eliminate the submissive and nervous body language that I was displaying when in the presence of women. I did that by getting rid of any 1) blocking behaviors, 2) self-soothing behaviors, and 3) negative facial expressions. Let me explain.

Blocking behavior

Blocking behavior happens when someone feels threatened, encounters a topic they don't like, or find themselves in a situation they can't control. People use blocking behavior to cover or block a part of their body as a barrier between them, someone, or something. Blocking behavior is used by people when they are troubled, feel disbelief, uncomfortable, vulnerable, worried, concerned, and nervous, or in disagreement. Examples of blocking behavior would be crossing your hands in front of your genitals (unconsciously protecting your vital organs), holding your drink in front of your chest, or squinting, rubbing, or shielding your eyes to block out and not be able to see what you do not like. Blocking behavior indicates we are feeling threatened and vulnerable.

Self-soothing behavior

Self-soothing behavior, or pacifying behavior, happens when someone is trying to calm themselves down or self-soothe. As young children, we would engage in various self-soothing habits for sheer pleasure to manage separations, new or uncomfortable situations, or distressing feelings. Examples would be thumb-sucking, rubbing, rocking, stroking, or head-banging. As adults, we will self-stroke in various non-sexual ways to calm ourselves down. An example would be touching or stroking the arms or rubbing palms together, nail-biting, rubbing hands on thighs, cracking fingers, licking lips, running our tongue over our teeth and, the man's favorite, back-of-the-neck rubbing. In case you are wondering, the women's favorite self-soothing is using fingers to cover their neck dimple and playing with their hair.

Your neck is one of the most vulnerable parts of the body. Neck touching or stroking is one of the most frequent pacifying behaviors we men use in responding to stress or uncomfortable situations. Self-soothing behavior or pacifying behavior indicates we are feeling nervous and unsure.

People tend to pick up and understand, although on an unconscious level, that when we are displaying self-soothing and blocking behavior, we are feeling uncomfortable and unsure about the situation. Trying to eliminate or at least reduce these behaviors will significantly improve how others perceive you.

Negative facial expressions

When we experience fear, stress, anger, displeasure, and disgust, our facial expressions are the first parts of the body to show this. We tend to tighten our jaw, squint with the eyes, and compress, or tighten our lips; all are signs of discomfort. Nervous and tense people also tend to blink frequently. These facial expressions should be avoided or controlled to show others that nothing can get under your skin.

Now you know what not to do, let's talk about body language you should utilize to appear more dominant, confident, and sure of your actions.

Relax

Relax – nothing is more important than you being relaxed. This is the foundation of conveying self-confidence and dominance. You should be relaxed at all times, with everyone you interact with, no matter where you are. You must make a deliberate effort to relax whenever you feel anxious, tense, or unsure, which are all signs of a submissive mindset. And I will show you how to do just that.

Relaxing will make you:

- More alert. Instead of frantically moving about and trying to gain people's attention, you can now sit back and observe your surroundings.

- Be aware of your emotions and make you think before you act. Any outside stimulus (an annoying co-worker, angry boss, a demanding woman) won't hold sway over your emotions (or at least you will think twice before expressing them). You will tend to respond rather than react.

- More charming and attractive. Because you're more relaxed, your personality shines through. Women are drawn to this kind of energy because it puts them at ease.

- Live in the present. You don't daydream, nor dwell too much in the past. Your entire focus is dedicated to what is currently happening.

- Overcome your flight-or-fight instincts. It's normal to be stressed whenever you find yourself in a tight spot. It's this stress that activates our primitive instincts to run away from the situation or fight it. By relaxing, you can take a step back and handle the situation with ease and make better, rational decisions.

- More confident. The two will always intersect; you can't have one without the other. Whenever you're nervous, it means that you don't have confidence in whatever you are doing. Women and people, in general, will pick up on this and find you less pleasant to be around.

The first step to becoming internally relaxed is getting your breathing under control. Take control of your breathing by using your diaphragm. Diaphragmatic breathing has a ton of benefits. It's known to help manage the symptoms of conditions such as irritable bowel syndrome, depression, anxiety, and sleeplessness.

Diaphragmatic breathing, sometimes called belly breathing, is useful because it has been shown to lower the heart rate, blood pressure, and the harmful effects of the stress hormone cortisol. It helps people to cope with the symptoms of post-traumatic stress disorder (PTSD), improve their core muscle stability, improve the body's ability to tolerate the intense exercise, and slows the rate of breathing so that it expends less energy. It is considered the most efficient way to breathe.

For the alpha male, one of the most significant benefits of diaphragmatic breathing is reducing stress and putting your body in a relaxed mode. You do this by making sure that your stomach is moving outward, and your chest remains relatively still while taking a breath.

Relaxing your mind

Stop worrying that much. Remember, you can't control what other people think or feel. You can only control yourself and the meaning you give to circumstances. So relax, enjoy yourself, and focus on the now and the big picture. No matter what happens in your life, you will be fine. Hey, you survived this far! When recalling the past, learn from it and move on. There is no reason to worry about it since it doesn't exist anymore.

"Worrying is like paying a debt you don't owe."
— Mark Twain

While practicing diaphragmatic breathing, put in the effort to purposefully relax by relaxing your muscles in your body and your eyes. That means no nervous jerky, twitchy movements, and darting around with your eyes. Re-fucking-lax. Relax your eyelids, only look at the things you are interested in. Relax your facial muscles and shoulders. Have a smile on your face if you wish. Don't be tense.

Eyes

The second most important indicator of your status and dominance is your eyes. Your eyes are more than just organs of your visual system. They can be used to change perceptions and create powerful emotions and feelings.

In general, people tend to look longer and more frequently at people or objects they like. A person may be trying to look uninterested and indifferent, but his/her eyes will keep returning to the object that attracts him/her. The same applies to people we like or find attractive.

Dominant and high-status men aren't afraid to look at people directly in the eye. Whenever you avert your gaze, you're exhibiting submissiveness. Looking down will give away your self-consciousness, embarrassment, your low standing, or possibly untrustworthy character.

When you enter a room, keep your eyes level and look people in the eyes as you greet them. The first person to look down is always the submissive person, so, when greeting others, don't look down or break eye contact, no matter how nervous or uncomfortable you feel. You must let the other person look away first. Try to maintain eye contact whenever you're conversing with someone. The results of a recent study have concluded that listeners perceive a talker's dominance when they keep eye contact during the conversation. When you're on the listening side, though, you do the opposite. The less you look at or give your attention to the person talking, the more you assert your dominance.

Follow these tips on good eye contact:

- Blink slowly and sexually. Relax your eyelids.
- When you talk or answer a question, **look directly at people's eyes.** Don't look down, to the left, right, up, or down.
- When others are talking, look away.
- **Do not stare** like a beta male who hasn't seen a woman in ages.
- On the street, lock eyes with women and have a genuine, sexy smile on your face.
- Your eye contact with your fellow men doesn't really matter. You shouldn't care how other men perceive you. Only look at them when you're saying something, but when they talk to you, avert your gaze.

- When walking, keep your eyes level.
- Learn to smile with your eyes. Practice this in the mirror. When your eyes smile, the outer corners of your eyes begin to wrinkle as muscles push them together.
- Practice making eye contact every single day.

Voice

Alphas use loud and deep voices to get their point across. This means no mumbling or using a quiet, soft, and high-pitched voice. When people feel uncertain or insecure, they tend to lower their voices, speaker faster, or speak with a higher pitch than usual in hopes no one will really hear them. They do this because they believe that what they are saying isn't really important or worth listening to. This is normal behavior for people who are afraid of being judged. Not you, though. Not anymore. Talk slowly and relaxed. Take your time. People are there to follow and listen to you—no need to rush.

Body

Finally, you have to control how you move your body. Alphas take up space with their bodies when they are sitting or standing. This means you can't be afraid of the so-called manspreading. Spread your legs to display your crotch proudly.

Take up space and "mark your territory" with your arms, elbows, legs, chest, and head. Lean back, keep your head high and claim your personal space, the more, the better. Expose the weakest and most vulnerable part of your body; your neck. When people come into your own space, make sure they know it. Be open; don't use your body to block or for self-soothing. Don't touch your face, neck, or legs. People who are unsure of themselves tend to make themselves as small as possible by occupying very little space. They are unconsciously trying to hide or remove themselves from the situation.

Mark your territory with your arms. Claim that armrest by resting your arm on it, or rest your arm around a chair, or on a table. The more confident or high-status individuals are, the more territory they claim with their arms, than less confident, lower-status individuals.

When you are standing, roll your shoulders back and push your chest out, taking up as much space as possible with the middle of your body. Make yourself as tall as possible, and keep your head high at all times. This shows that you are proud of your body and comfortable in your   skin.

It may sound silly but try always to stand higher than the other person. Put yourself in a dominant position that allows you to keep your body higher than the other person. This gives you a natural advantage and makes you appear more authoritative and dominant. An example would be standing while the other person is sitting.

Things to avoid:

- Do NOT smile too much, and for no reason. Even in the behavior of primates, the betas will smile to convey their submission towards the alphas. Just like the beta primates, beta males will smile to show that they're no threat.
- Do NOT slouch or have a closed and timid posture.
- Do NOT take up as little physical space as possible. This indicates nervousness and your low standing.
- Do NOT walk and move without a purpose. Every gesture you use should have a function. Otherwise, don't use it.

Try to grow out of your nervous ticks and self-soothing behavior (i.e., playing with your hair, playing with your pen, drumming with your fingers). Especially when you are with a woman.

Aggression and dominance are two entirely different things. Showing dominance will make people respect you while showing aggression will make people afraid of you, or even think you are unhinged. Learn the difference.

You have to be selective with your body language. Being too dominant when in the presence of other men will likely not make you any new friends, but display the right amount of dominance and you may gain some new followers. It's all about context. Displaying too dominant body language while applying for a new job might give the wrong message or even insult the person interviewing you. Be smart about it. When you are on a date or alone with a woman, the more relaxed body language you display, with a pinch of dominance, the better.

The four key fundamentals of this chapter:

- Re-fucking-lax! Remember to breathe with your abdomen, not your chest. Not being relaxed while displaying other dominant behavior may convey a more aggressive message. Relax!
- Eyes, they never lie. Practice eye-contact.
- When talking, use a deep, calm voice. Take your time when speaking.
- Spread out your body and use slow, well-thought-out movements.

Women's Body Language

The most important body parts when trying to decipher female body language are her eyes, lips, neck, and palms. Females who like you will display submissive and relaxed body language. Females who are afraid of you will display submissive but defensive body language. And females who don't like you and are not afraid of you will display dominant, aggressive, and defensive body language. It's essential to know the difference.

You want her to display relaxed and submissive body language. Change something up when you notice she is getting defensive but remains submissive. Leave her alone if she is showing dominant, aggressive, and defensive body language.

When women feel comfortable and sexy, they **expose** their throats, **tilt** their necks, **touch** themselves, **reveal** their palms and wrists, **show off** their breasts, and have and pre-orgasmic facial expressions. Remember these! When you are on a date or with a woman, and when you see these signs, it means the date is going well, and her Genuine Attraction for you is increasing.

When women don't like a particular situation they are in, or when they are nervous, they usually compress their lips, dart with their eyes all over the place, and have a closed-off posture by unconsciously protecting themselves and their internal organs. Especially their neck and throat.

If you notice that a woman is increasingly showing more negative body language, awkward facial expressions, or self-soothing behavior, make her feel more comfortable by first purposefully relaxing her body through breathing and taking control of the situation. That will indirectly have a relaxing effect on her.

Note! Not everything she does is the result of your behavior or what you said. People are always thinking, so you can't take it personally when a woman is occasionally showing self-soothing behavior or negative facial expressions. This only becomes a problem when it's constant, and her verbal communication matches her nonverbal communication.

"At their core, feminine women would rather spend five minutes with a true alpha male, than have a lifetime of love, devotion, and commitment from a beta male."

—- Stevan Terzić

Part 7: Love and Long-term Relationships

Love

You might be thinking that this chapter is going in a different direction from the rest of what I've taught you, but I'll have to disappoint you. Let me tell you something – love *is* essential! It's one of the most beautiful emotions a human can ever experience in their life.

In the eyes of a true alpha, this quote sums it up, pretty well:

"You must love in such a way that the other person feels free."
— Thich Nhat Hanh

If you remember it right, alpha males are in total and utter control of themselves and not in the control of other people. There is nothing more frustrating than being in a relationship based on rules.

When two individuals, one of them being a beta male, begin a relationship, they set their rules and boundaries that the other has to follow. Failing to follow through with these "requests" results in an argument or even a breakup. Some common rules are listed below.

- You shall not text any other men/women.
- You shall not go out every Saturday.
- You shall not wear any revealing clothes.
- You shall not buy that car/toy/computer.
- You shall not flirt with other people.
- You shall not have sex with other people.
- You shall always let me know where you are and what you are up to.

That doesn't sound like love to me. It sounds more like a prison, which eventually you or she will want to break free from.

What happens if she breaks some of your rules? You become upset and try to straighten things out with her, but how often does it end amicably? Odds are, she'll just fight back, deepening the problem instead of resolving it. What if she violates one of your most important rules? Wouldn't you feel hurt and angry?

In most cases, you would. A relationship shouldn't be constricted by rules and regulations. As Thich Nhat Hanh aptly puts it, your love is supposed to liberate your partner, not imprison them. This is the philosophy I want you to live by.

You can't control other people, nor should you want to. Beta males love to believe they are in control of other people. The problem is that if you want to control someone, you will need to watch their every move. You shouldn't have or even take time for that. That's time wasted.

Never enter a relationship with a woman if they start imposing rules that constrict your freedom. The same principle applies to you. Leave your partner to do whatever she wants. We, red-pill alphas, base our relationships on standards, not rules.

Sex

Humans might just be the most sexual creature ever to walk this earth. Sex isn't just a means of reproduction for us. It's a source of pleasure and ultimate satisfaction. Sex is essential, not just for men, but for women as well. It should be a part of your regular routine. It's the most physically pleasurable thing a human can experience. Nothing really tops it. Granted, other aspects of our life could be seen as more satisfying and enjoyable, but those lean more on the psychological and spiritual side of things, not the physical.

A sexually vital and healthy human desires some sexual variety. In fact, variety (uncertainty) is one of our primal human needs. Even back in prehistoric times, the alpha gets their pick of the best mates in his tribe, and this has been the status quo for several millennia. Nature discourages us from mating with our family members (notice the genetic defects of products of incest.) This is why we desire to mate with other women who aren't part of our household, making them better choices to bear our offspring.

This is also why sexually vital men tend to move on from one woman to the next, fairly quickly. The moment they become a part of our "family"/"tribe," and the deep connection is established, and our need for certainty and connection are adequately met, we are wired to find another mate, even if we carry deep feelings for them. In fact, I have noticed that the more I genuinely cared and developed deep feelings for a woman, the less sexually attractive she became to me. It was Sigmund Freud who noticed and pointed out our difficulties connecting love with sexual desire in an essay titled '*On the Universal Tendency to Debasement in the Sphere of Love.*'

He wrote: '*Where they love, they have no desire, and where they desire, they cannot love.*'

Odds are, you've probably already felt these desires at some point in your life. Whenever you get into a serious long-term relationship or even eventually get married, no matter how wonderful or beautiful she is, no matter how much you love and care for her, there will come a time when you will desire another. This is entirely acceptable and normal, especially when you take into consideration our six core human needs. This need for a change, thrill, and excitement isn't as wrong or selfish as the blue-pilled world might portray. Trying to suppress these desires will only lead to your downfall and unhappiness.

Long-term Relationship

There are instances where men do want to settle with a woman and form a life-long relationship, and this is completely fine too. As long as it's not an act of desperation, stemming from loneliness or wanting to settle or feel complete, then this is a reasonable goal to want. Especially when we get older, and the chances of actually mating with the fit women we genuinely desire, are getting slim as the days go by. Another perfectly good reason to get into a monogamous marriage, and promise yourself to one woman, is if your sex drive is extremely low. Third, and the best, reason to get into a monogamous marriage would be if you have found a woman who can meet a high number of your core human needs, and she has proved this for a certain period of time (two years or longer).

Any other purposes for marrying a woman are imposed on men from within our blue-pilled society and shouldn't be taken into consideration. Examples would be; you have to get married for a happy life, you have to get married before your forties, etc.

I believe that a man can form a lasting relationship with someone if:

- Both parties put zero or very few rules on the relationship.
- There is mutual respect.
- S/he knows her/his role as prescribed by her/his gender.
- She places a high priority on sex.
- She places a high priority on communication.
- She is flexible, fun and playful.
- They avoid boring "routines."
- There aren't too many incompatibilities between the two.
- They share similar values.

- She can meet two or more of his core needs.
- He can meet two or more of her core needs.
- She supports a man's vision, purpose, and mission.
- He keeps dating her even after they have been in a relationship or marriage for many years.
- They have fun together.
- They have frequent and fulfilling sex.

You will never find a woman that you are entirely compatible with. The trick is to find someone with **positive traits that outweigh the negative** and someone **whose core values match yours.**

There are ways you can work towards a long relationship working in tandem, as long as they don't sacrifice your identity or lead you away from your purpose. Changing yourself for the sake of another person is unreasonable. Some change can be useful if you're sure that it turns you into a better man in the long run, but it must be your decision, and no one else's. You should never compromise your integrity, values, and standards just to please other people.

Keep in mind, in a committed relationship, and especially when you decide to have children and want to get married, you will always have to sacrifice some things that make you an alpha male. Things like freedom, sleeping with other women, and being in total and utter control of your life. If you value connection or family more than liberty, I see no reasons why not to choose that lifestyle. There is no right or wrong here; it's highly personal and totally up to you.

Because connection and flexibility are key to a long-lasting relationship, you should get into a committed relationship with the following attitude: a relationship must be a place where you go to give, not to take, or need! I heard that one from Tony Robbins, and it makes perfect sense.

Attraction, sex, and lust are not enough to make a long-term relationship work. Sex and passion can't fulfill all human needs sufficiently. You need connection and love. And if your values don't match, and one or both of you can't, or don't want to, meet each other's standards, think twice before making a commitment and entering into a monogamous relationship or marriage.

Before Making a Commitment

Before popping the question, you have to be absolutely sure the woman you want to marry is flexible, has the same attitude when it comes to a relationship (a place to give and not to take), and shares the same, or very similar, values as you. **This behavior has to be consistent for at least two years or more.**

Almost 50% of every traditional Western marriage tends to fail, which results in separation, divorce, infidelity, or a toxic and inescapable relationship. An actual living hell, if you ask me. I believe the main reason for this high divorce rate could be explained by looking back and figuring out whose idea it was to get married in the first place.

Relationships and marriages MUST be women's ideas. If a man insists on marrying a woman, without her explicitly asking for it, that marriage or long-term relationship is doomed to fail. Men try to corner women into marrying, believing that with time, marriage will increase their Genuine Attraction for him. It never does; it only drops it even further.

*"I do not think you can name many great inventions
that have been made by married men."*
— Nikola Tesla

Breaking Up

When your Genuine Attraction for her drops, be honest with yourself and with her. Tell her that you want to separate and go your own way.

No matter how "special" someone might be, you can always move on and get attracted to and get connected with someone else. Just think of how many divorced or widowed people that you know or heard of, got remarried. Most people *choose* not to move on and believe with their whole hearts in "The One" myth. Because people's belief in "The One" is so strong, they tend to suffer by staying in unhealthy, unfulfilling, and sexless relationships for long periods, even if their partner has lost almost all of their Genuine Attraction for them.

Cheating

Don't cheat; it's weak and devious behavior. I assume being devious, lying, and cheating doesn't align with your core values, so you shouldn't do it. If you want to have sex with multiple women, simply don't get into a serious monogamous relationship. You have to live your truth.

Getting Back Together

If she dumped you, her Genuine Attraction dropped below 4.9. That means it's over, it is done forget about it. Move on. It will never be the same. Do not try to get her back. Why? The benefit you'll gain will be significantly outweighed by what you'd have to put up with. I have said this multiple times already because I want you to memorize it. It's not worth it.

If you've dumped her, well, I assume you broke up with her for a reason. She did something to make you mad, disappointed, and to get you that far, you felt like you needed to break up with her. This tells me she is either devious, untrustworthy, has no integrity, or a combination of those (assuming you've read her Genuine Attraction for you correctly).

Whatever the case might be, the benefit you'll gain will be significantly outweighed by what you'd have to put up with.

When Facing A Divorce

Shut up and document. That's all I got to say.

"It's not what you know; it's what you can prove."

— Alonzo, Training Day

The eight key fundamentals of this chapter:

- Love is supposed to liberate you and your partner, not imprison you or your partner.
- Relationships must be based on standards, not rules.
- It is natural to desire and have sex with many women.
- You will never find a woman that you are entirely compatible with. The trick is to find someone with positive traits that outweigh the negative and someone whose core values match yours.
- Only marry flexible women. This flexible behavior has to be consistent for at least two years.
- Never stay in an unhappy relationship.
- Don't take your ex back. The benefit you'll gain will be significantly outweighed by what you'd have to put up with.
- If you are facing a divorce, shut up and document.

Part 8: Your Purpose In Life

There is a slim chance that you already have a mission in your life: a purpose that motivates your everyday existence, something that you dedicate most of your energy to. Few people already have a clear idea of what they want. Chances are, your life doesn't have a precise direction yet. True, you might already have some strong aspirations and convictions, and that's a good start. You may have already lived a life full of experience, which made your likes and your dislikes all the more apparent. That's all well and good, but all those things you've done don't even come close to what your TRUE purpose is.

Your life's true purpose should encompass all of your actions and your whole existence. It's literally the purpose of your life. You're probably familiar with the "purpose/mission" statements most companies have to motivate their workforce. Your purpose has basically the same function; only you don't just uphold it during your work, you practice it in every aspect of your life. It's that reason that you get up every morning. It's the thing that drives you to learn new things, work your hardest, push yourself to the limits, fail, and learn from your mistakes. This is the catalyst for all your actions.

Don't be confused between your purpose and your goals. While both can intersect with each other, there is a clear difference between them, that everyone should know about. A goal is specific, measurable, attainable, realistic, and time-bounded. Afterward, it's basically finished. Goals have an ending to them; your purpose does not. Different goals must be achieved to fulfill your life purpose. The purpose is something that you aspire to your whole life. It's not something that can be done in one sitting, a day or even a year, like a goal. More often than not, it takes a whole lifetime for an average person to accomplish their purpose.

To give you a more apparent distinction between your goals and your purpose, a goal can be changed, discarded, or forgotten. Your purpose, on the other hand, cannot, because it is a part of you. It's intrinsic to who you are as a person.

For example, a great goal is, "I'm going to lose x amount of weight over the course of two years. I will work out five days a week, eat a clean diet, and get at least eight hours of sleep every day."

While you can tweak your purpose by just a bit if ever the need arises, at its innermost core, it is unyielding and constant. You commit to it your whole life. Nothing should stand in the way of your purpose, and nothing should take precedence over it. Even if it's your lover or your wife that's dissuading you from your purpose, never falter. If you do, then you've probably never had a real purpose in the first place.

Your purpose is not an obligation towards another person. Like I've said before, your purpose is about YOU. It's how you work towards yourself and your life, and no one else. This might seem selfish at first, but remember, no one is stopping you from helping the people you love as well, just don't let your goals (helping people is a great goal) cloud your purpose.

How to find your purpose and mission in life:

Passion vs. Abilities

Find what you have a passion for! Passion is the catalyst or the spark that sets off the rest of your actions. It's your pool of energy and power that you should utilize to make the hurdles in your life a bit easier. It's the invisible helping hand that pushes you towards the right path. Your passion feels natural to you, and like something you are supposed to be doing and spending your time on. Besides, you will be damn good at it! Sounds all fine and dandy, typical blue-pilled advice.

Sadly, most people won't have the ability, courage, and perseverance to make something from their passion. In order to turn your passion into your profession, you'll probably need a coach. And most people aren't willing to hire a coach, so most people fail to turn their passion into their profession or career, and will never be able to make any income from their passion. So they will suffer, struggle, and never achieve true happiness and fulfillment.

You should instead focus on your skills, abilities, assess your strengths, and identify needs in the market. That way, you will seize the opportunity, and along the way, you might become passionate about something you never thought you would.

"If you trust in yourself...and believe in your dreams...
and follow your star...you'll still get beaten by people who spent
their time working hard and learning things and weren't so lazy."
— Terry Pratchett

Don't get me wrong; it's great if you have a passion for something, and it's even better if you can make something out of it; just don't waste your precious and limited time. This doesn't mean you should get rid of the things you are passionate about. In fact, you must keep developing your passions, so when the opportunity arises, you'll be ready to seize it.

If you are really, absolutely determined, and I wholeheartedly encourage you to be, go for it! But be sure to hire a coach, someone who can push you beyond your limits and help you become everything that you ever wanted to be.

But you better be ready to give it your all with your body, mind, and soul. That way, you are setting yourself up for success.

*"Our dreams and passions don't always correspond
with our destinies, and it is our destinies that
might fulfill us more than our dreams ever could."*
— Stevan Terzić

*"You don't choose your passions;
your passions choose you."*
— Jeff Bezos

**Your purpose depends on your desires,
hard work, actions, and dedication.**

Therefore it is not something that should be dependent on things you cannot control, like another person or even a specific group of people. Your purpose cannot rely on other people. Everyone and this also includes the people you hold affection for (i.e., your wife, kids), is not something you should rely on as holding their relevance your whole life. People are highly dynamic creatures and often change their minds, the places they live, and their life choices. What happens if your purpose depends on someone that moves to another continent? What happens if that person dies? What then? If you make them your purpose, you will only reach an inevitable and undesirable dead end. Your purpose must be more prominent and greater than that.

Your purpose must be aligned with your core values. Your core values and personal standards are things that are valuable and most important to you and influence every aspect of your life. All of your decisions are based on your core values. Enjoyable life is one where your core values form the basis of all your decisions, and your personal standards enforce those core values. If your decisions are not aligned with your core values, a life of misery and resentment is bound to happen.

Your purpose must help you achieve
a higher level of fulfillment.

In order to achieve that, your purpose must meet at least the last two of the six human needs; growth and contribution. That means your purpose must push you to grow mentally, emotionally, and spiritually, and it must offer significant value to others by improving the position of others.

Growth and contribution are only two of the six core human needs and, unlike some of the other needs, are not in conflict with each other.

By contributing, focusing on giving back, and helping others meet their own needs, you actually meet all of the six other core human needs in the process.

You see, as a red-pill man, you should prioritize fulfillment above happiness. Happiness is temporary, and it tends to be externally triggered and is primarily based on other people, places, thoughts, things, and events.

Fulfillment is consistent and is cultivated internally. That's why it can only be achieved by people with an internal locus of control.

Happiness comes through us getting, while fulfillment comes through us giving. You get happy when you get a new car, more money, a new house, etc. You get fulfilled when you contribute and give to others.

The secret to living a fulfilled life is giving. Contributing to the greater good usually reflects how you feel about yourself and how you feel about others. Unhappy and troubled people are rarely contributing without a hidden motive.

What if none of your core values includes contribution or growth? In the U.S. alone, 70% of people working are unhappy and don't care about what they do.[5] Most people live an unfulfilling life. Re-evaluate your core values and determine what is really important to you.

Your purpose in life should make you money.

You should look for a way to earn money through your purpose while offering significant value to others. I emphasize the word should because your purpose doesn't necessarily have to make you money. Think about monks, who clearly have a defined fulfilling purpose in their life and are some of the happiest and peaceful men in the world. But, since you are looking to become more alpha and the purpose of this book is to help you become just that, money is essential. Try to emulate other successful people you know by using their business model as a source of inspiration.

This way, you're already setting yourself up for success. It is okay if you've not found a way to monetize your purpose yet, but you should never stop trying to achieve that goal. In the meantime, try to make as much money as possible while contributing to society.

The Thing About Money…

There are two main and legal ways to make money in the world. For the first, one has to play the corporate game where you accomplish your tasks and follow orders to a T. Something I hate with a passion, and I want nothing to do with it. Most of the business focus is on making profit only, while simultaneously one of the core objectives is to beat the competition, rather than actually contributing to society. A job provides a somewhat steady income and a false sense of security. And with a bit of "luck," you'll get promoted.

---

[5] https://www.charities.org/news/majority-us-employees-not-engaged-despite-gains-2014

Office politics is a must; kissing your boss's ass and backstabbing your co-workers is the only way to rise in rank. This isn't exactly a favorable scenario, even for people with just an ounce of self-worth.

The other way is a high risk/reward situation where you take your shot, a calculated risk, and an educated decision, and try to form your very own business or invest and make your money work for you.

Will money make you happy? Maybe, maybe not, but the lack of it will definitely make you miserable. You don't have to be rich, whatever that means, just have your finances in order. Make comfort, enjoyment of life, and financial security, on your terms, some of the top priorities in your life. How much money you need depends on your needs and your environment.

Money is only an exchange of value, and it will only give you options. These options will provide you with choices in life that people with no money don't have. Alphas have the choice; betas don't. Money is a tool, a means to an end, and should never be the end in itself. Most people who have grown up poor, tend to make accumulating money or cutting costs, one of their life's missions, not realizing that most of the time, they just want to fulfill their need for certainty.

To get more options in life, you need to have enough money in the bank. That's a fact of life. Just don't become a modern-day economic slave, because chasing money, for the sake of accumulating it, always comes with a high cost. Making money is a great goal, but it shouldn't be your primary purpose in life.

Always stay focused on achieving your life purpose. Do not let distractions turn into excuses. Someday is not a day of the week, and it never will be. Sometimes 'later' becomes 'never. Stay away from the things and people in life that hinder you in fulfilling your life purpose.

Take your time and think about your purpose, because in the process of fulfilling your life purpose, you will have to sacrifice some things in your life. But in the end, it will not matter, since you will live for your mission.

Having a purpose and staying on it, no matter what happens, is one of the most masculine traits you can possess. Look at the most successful people in the world and examine their missions and purpose in life. Don't copy and paste since other people have a different perspective on life, different desires, and needs, and they live in a different environment to you, but try to learn from them and adapt their strategies into your life.

The five key fundamentals of this chapter:

- Focus on your abilities, assess your strengths, and identify needs in the market. Stay on the lookout for your next passion, and keep developing your current ones.
- Your purpose depends on YOUR desires, hard work, action, and dedication. It shouldn't depend on things you cannot control, like a specific person or even a particular group of people.
- Your purpose must help you achieve a higher level of fulfillment.
- Your purpose should make you money.
- Always, no matter what, stay at your purpose. Do not let distractions turn into excuses.

Conclusion

Once you become a man who is true to himself, one who is in charge of his own destiny, someone who lives life without regrets, and is driven by his purpose—when you become the best version of yourself—you will find that you're becoming genuinely happy, fulfilled and you'll finally get the things you want in life, love and sex. You won't need other peoples' approval.

This book was about much more than just dating and women. It's about living your life passionately, full of adventurers and experiences.

Listen to your heart and go after the things you want in life. Don't ever let someone tell you that you can't do something. Never apologize for being yourself. You have a limited time here on this rock, so try to make the most of it. When it comes to women, keep these things in mind:

1. Don't get lost in self-analysis by trying to understand and justify everything you think and do. You don't have to dissect your every thought and action, just have fun and be yourself. After you have studied this material thoroughly, things will come naturally.
2. You must, at all times, create your own strong and positive reality and pull her into it. Control the meaning you give to events.
3. When you become a high-value man, you don't need women's approval.
4. My final piece of advice is this, never devote yourself completely to any woman. Learn to embrace being alone.

Now, go out there and live life on your **own** terms. Don't wait. The time will never be just right.

To get a better grasp of these concepts, join my weekly life-changing, exclusive content in form of a newsletter email which you will benefit from your entire life. This membership includes coaching through email.

Join now by signing up at **DatingAfterTheRedPill.com**

Stevan Terzić

"Life is very short and anxious for those who forget the past, neglect the present, and fear the future."
— Seneca

Made in the USA
Coppell, TX
26 February 2022